THE ANNOTATED LUTHER STUDY EDITION

# The Freedom of a Christian

## 1520

THE ANNOTATED LUTHER STUDY EDITION

# The Freedom
# of a Christian

## 1520

TIMOTHY J. WENGERT

Fortress Press
Minneapolis

*The Freedom of a Christian, 1520*
THE ANNOTATED LUTHER STUDY EDITION

Excerpted from The Annotated Luther, Volume 1, *The Roots of Reform*
(Minneapolis: Fortress Press, 2015), Timothy J. Wengert, volume editor.

Fortress Press Publication Staff:
Scott Tunseth, Project Editor
Marissa Wold Uhrina, Production Manager
Laurie Ingram, Cover Design
Esther Diley, Permissions

Copyeditor: David Lott
Series design and typesetting: Ann Delgehausen, Trio Bookworks
Proofreader: Laura Weller

Library of Congress Cataloging-in-Publication Data is available

Print ISBN: 978-1-5064-1351-8
eISBN: 978-1-5064-1352-5

The paper used in this publication meets the minimum requirements of American National Standard for Information Sciences—Permanence of Paper for Printed Library Materials, ANSI Z329, 48-1984.

Manufactured in the U.S.A.

# Contents

*Publisher's Note about The Annotated Luther Study Edition*   vii

*Series Introduction*   ix

*Abbreviations*   xiii

Introduction                                                    467

The Freedom of a Christian, 1520                                474

*Image Credits*   539

# Publisher's Note

## About the Annotated Luther Study Edition

The volumes in the Annotated Luther Study Edition series have first been published in one of the comprehensive volumes of The Annotated Luther series. A description of that series and the volumes can be found in the Series Introduction (p. vii). While each comprehensive Annotated Luther volume can easily be used in classroom settings, we also recognize that treatises are often assigned individually for reading and study. To facilitate classroom and group use, we have pulled key treatises along with their introductions, annotations, and images directly from the Annotated Luther Series volumes.

Please note that the study edition page numbers match the page numbers of the larger Annotated Luther volume in which it first appeared. We have intentionally retained the same page numbering to facilitate use of the study editions and larger volumes side by side.

*The Freedom of a Christian, 1520,*
was first published in The Annotated Luther series,
Volume 1, *The Roots of Reform* (2015).

# Series Introduction

## Engaging the Essential Luther

Even after five hundred years Martin Luther continues to engage and challenge each new generation of scholars and believers alike. With 2017 marking the five-hundredth anniversary of Luther's *95 Theses*, Luther's theology and legacy are being explored around the world with new questions and methods and by diverse voices. His thought invites ongoing examination, his writings are a staple in classrooms and pulpits, and he speaks to an expanding assortment of conversation partners who use different languages and hale from different geographical and social contexts.

The six volumes of The Annotated Luther edition offer a flexible tool for the global reader of Luther, making many of his most important writings available in the *lingua franca* of our times as one way of facilitating interest in the Wittenberg reformer. They feature new introductions, annotations, revised translations, and textual notes, as well as visual enhancements (illustrations, art, photos, maps, and timelines). The Annotated Luther edition embodies Luther's own cherished principles of communication. Theological writing, like preaching, needs to reflect human beings' lived experience, benefits from up-to-date scholarship, and should be easily accessible to all. These volumes are designed to help teachers and students, pastors and laypersons, and other professionals in ministry understand the context in which the documents were written, recognize how the documents have shaped Protestant and Lutheran thinking, and interpret the meaning of these documents for faith and life today.

## The Rationale for This Edition

For any reader of Luther, the sheer number of his works presents a challenge. Well over one hundred volumes comprise the scholarly edition of Luther's works, the so-called Weimar Ausgabe (WA), a publishing enterprise begun in 1883 and only completed in the twenty-first century. From 1955 to 1986, fifty-five volumes came to make up *Luther's Works* (American Edition) (LW), to which Concordia Publishing House, St. Louis, is adding still more. This English-language contribution to Luther studies, matched by similar translation projects for Erasmus of Rotterdam and John Calvin, provides a theological and historical gold mine for those interested in studying Luther's thought. But even these volumes are not always easy to use and are hardly portable. Electronic forms have increased availability, but preserving Luther in book form and providing readers with manageable selections are also important goals.

Moreover, since the publication of the WA and the first fifty-five volumes of the LW, research on the Reformation in general and on Martin Luther in particular has broken new ground and evolved, as has knowledge regarding the languages in which Luther wrote. Up-to-date information from a variety of sources is brought together in The Annotated Luther, building on the work done by previous generations of scholars. The language and phrasing of the translations have also been updated to reflect modern English usage. While the WA and, in a derivative way, LW remain the central source for Luther scholarship, the present critical and annotated English translation facilitates research internationally and invites a new generation of readers for whom Latin and German might prove an unsurpassable obstacle to accessing Luther. The WA provides the basic Luther texts (with some exceptions); the LW provides the basis for almost all translations.

## Defining the "Essential Luther"

Deciding which works to include in this collection was not easy. Criteria included giving attention to Luther's initial key works; considering which publications had the most impact in his day and later; and taking account of Luther's own favorites, texts addressing specific issues of continued importance for today, and Luther's exegetical works. Taken as a whole, these works present the many sides of Luther, as reformer, pastor, biblical interpreter, and theologian. To serve today's readers and by using categories similar to those found in volumes 31–47 of Luther's works (published by Fortress Press), the volumes offer in the main a thematic rather than strictly chronological approach to Luther's writings. The volumes in the series include:

> Volume 1: *The Roots of Reform* (Timothy J. Wengert, editor)
> Volume 2: *Word and Faith* (Kirsi I. Stjerna, editor)
> Volume 3: *Church and Sacraments* (Paul W. Robinson, editor)
> Volume 4: *Pastoral Writings* (Mary Jane Haemig, editor)
> Volume 5: *Christian Life in the World* (Hans J. Hillerbrand, editor)
> Volume 6: *The Interpretation of Scripture* (Euan K. Cameron, editor)

## The History of the Project

In 2011 Fortress Press convened an advisory board to explore the promise and parameters of a new English edition of Luther's essential works. Board members Denis Janz, Robert Kolb, Peter Matheson, Christine Helmer, and Kirsi Stjerna deliberated with

Fortress Press publisher Will Bergkamp to develop a concept and identify contributors. After a review with scholars in the field, college and seminary professors, and pastors, it was concluded that a single-language edition was more desirable than dual-language volumes.

In August 2012, Hans Hillerbrand, Kirsi Stjerna, and Timothy Wengert were appointed as general editors of the series with Scott Tunseth from Fortress Press as the project editor. The general editors were tasked with determining the contents of the volumes and developing the working principles of the series. They also helped with the identification and recruitment of additional volume editors, who in turn worked with the general editors to identify volume contributors. Mastery of the languages and unique knowledge of the subject matter were key factors in identifying contributors. Most contributors are North American scholars and native English speakers, but The Annotated Luther includes among its contributors a circle of international scholars. Likewise, the series is offered for a global network of teachers and students in seminary, university, and college classes, as well as pastors, lay teachers, and adult students in congregations seeking background and depth in Lutheran theology, biblical interpretation, and Reformation history.

## Editorial Principles

The volume editors and contributors have, with few exceptions, used the translations of LW as the basis of their work, retranslating from the WA for the sake of clarity and contemporary usage. Where the LW translations have been substantively altered, explanatory notes have often been provided. More importantly, contributors have provided marginal notes to help readers understand theological and historical references. Introductions have been expanded and sharpened to reflect the very latest historical and theological research. In citing the Bible, care has been taken to reflect the German and Latin texts commonly used in the sixteenth century rather than modern editions, which often employ textual sources that were unavailable to Luther and his contemporaries.

Finally, all pieces in The Annotated Luther have been revised in the light of modern principles of inclusive language. This is not always an easy task with a historical author, but an intentional effort has been made to revise language throughout, with creativity and editorial liberties, to allow Luther's theology to speak free from unnecessary and unintended gender-exclusive language. This important principle provides an opportunity to translate accurately certain gender-neutral German and Latin expressions that Luther employed—for example, the Latin word *homo* and the German *Mensch* mean "human being," not simply "males." Using the words *man* and *men* to translate such terms would create an ambiguity not present in the original texts. The focus is on linguistic accuracy and Luther's intent. Regarding creedal formulations and trinitarian language, Luther's own expressions have been preserved, without entering the complex and important contemporary debates over language for God and the Trinity.

The 2017 anniversary of the publication of the *95 Theses* is providing an opportunity to assess the substance of Luther's role and influence in the Protestant Reformation. Revisiting Luther's essential writings not only allows reassessment of Luther's rationale and goals but also provides a new look at what Martin Luther was about and why new generations would still wish to engage him. We hope these six volumes offer a compelling invitation.

Hans J. Hillerbrand
Kirsi I. Stjerna
Timothy J. Wengert
*General Editors*

# Abbreviations

| | |
|---|---|
| BC | *The Book of Concord*, ed. Robert Kolb and Timothy J. Wengert (Minneapolis: Fortress Press, 2000). |
| Brecht 1 | Martin Brecht, *Martin Luther: His Road to Reformation, 1483–1521*, trans. James L. Schaaf (Minneapolis: Fortress Press, 1985). |
| CA | *Augsburg Confession* |
| CR | *Corpus Reformatorum: Philippi Melanthonis opera quae supersunt omnia*, ed. Karl Brettschneider and Heinrich Bindseil, 28 vols. (Braunschweig: Schwetchke, 1834–1860). |
| DWB | *Deutsches Wörterbuch*, ed. Jakob and Wilhelm Grimm, 16 vols. in 32 parts (Leipzig, 1854–1960). |
| Friedberg | *Corpus iuris canonici*, ed. Emil Friedberg, 2 vols. (Leipzig: Tauchnitz, 1879–1881). |
| LC | *Large Catechism* |
| LW | *Luther's Works* (American edition), ed. Helmut Lehmann and Jaroslav Pelikan, 55 vols. (Philadelphia: Fortress Press/St. Louis: Concordia Publishing House, 1955–1986). |
| MLStA | *Martin Luther: Studienausgabe*, ed. Hans-Ulrich Delius, 6 vols. (Berlin/Leipzig: Evangelische Verlagsanstalt, 1979–1999). |
| MPL | *Patrologiae cursus completus, series Latina*, ed. Jacques-Paul Migne, 217 vols. (Paris, 1815–1875). |
| NPNF | *Nicene and Post-Nicene Fathers*, ed. Philip Schaaf and Henry Wace, series 1, 14 vols.; series 2, 14 vols. (London/New York: T&T Clark, 1886–1900). |
| RTA | Adolf Wrede et al., eds., *Deutsche Reichtagsakten, jüngere Reihe*, 20 vols. (Gotha: Perthes, 1893–2009). |
| WA | *Luthers Werke: Kritische Gesamtausgabe [Schriften]*, 73 vols. (Weimar: H. Böhlau, 1883–2009). |
| WA Br | *Luthers Werke: Kritische Gesamtausgabe: Briefwechsel*, 18 vols. (Weimar: H. Böhlau, 1930–1985). |
| WA DB | *Luthers Werke: Kritische Gesamtausgabe: Deutsche Bibel*, 12 vols. (Weimar: H. Böhlau, 1906–1961). |
| WA TR | *Luthers Werke: Kritische Gesamtausgabe: Tischreden*, 6 vols. (Weimar: H. Böhlau, 1912–1921). |
| Wander | Karl F. W. Wander, ed., *Deutsches Sprichwörterlexikon: Ein Hausschatz für das deutsche Volk*, 5 vols. (Leipzig: Brockhaus, 1867–1880; reprint Aalen: Scientia, 1963). |

# The Freedom of a Christian

## 1520

TIMOTHY J. WENGERT

## INTRODUCTION

The movement within Western Christianity that began in 1517 with the posting of Martin Luther's *95 Theses*, now known as the Reformation, was by no means a foregone conclusion in its earliest stages. Starting with the papal legate, Cardinal Cajetan's (1469–1534) interview of Luther in October 1518,[1] various attempts were made first to avoid or mitigate Luther's impending condemnation by the pope and, later, to find ways around the papal condemnation and the impending judgment of the imperial diet (parliament) that finally met in Worms in April 1521. One such embassy fell on the shoulders of Karl von Miltitz (c. 1490–1529), who throughout 1520 tried to find ways around the impasse between Luther and his supporters (along with his protector prince, the Elector Frederick of Saxony [1463–1525]) on the one side and the papal court and its defenders on the other.[2]

Luther left the final meeting with von Miltitz with instructions to write a reconciliation-minded letter to Pope Leo X (1475–1521), which he did in the weeks that followed and to which he appended a nonpolemical tract describing the heart of his beliefs. (Indeed, compared to other major tracts he produced in 1520, *The Freedom of a Christian* has

1. See above, pp. 121–65.

2. For the details of the historical record, see Brecht 1:400–415, and Berndt Hamm, *The Early Luther: Stages in a Reformation Reorientation* (Grand Rapids: Eerdmans, 2014), 172–89.

**3.** These tracts include two others in this volume, *Sermon on Good Works* and *Address to the Christian Nobility*, and *The Babylonian Captivity of the Church*, in LW 36:3–126.

**4.** Hamm, *The Early Luther*, 172–89.

**5.** For a translation of the German preface, see LW 31:333. For a translation of the entire German tract, see Philip Krey and Peter Krey, eds., *Luther's Spirituality* (Mahwah, NJ: Paulist, 2007), 69–90.

a remarkably temperate tone.)[3] The dedicatory letter to Leo X represents what might be called a "case study" in the proposal found in *The Freedom of a Christian*, where Luther shows both his deep respect for the pope and his surprising freedom in proclaiming the gospel. While it is clear that these two documents should, therefore, be read in tandem, several accidents of history allowed for their own separate existence.[4]

In September 1520, probably working from a detailed Latin outline, Luther first completed the German version of *The Freedom of a Christian* and its epistle dedicatory to Leo X. Because the letter to Leo X arrived first at the printer, however, Johann Grünenberg (d. c. 1525)—knowing a bestseller when he saw one—printed it separately, forcing Luther to write a second, perfunctory preface for the German version to Hermann Mühlpfort (c. 1486–1534), mayor of Zwickau. Thus, some copies of the German version of *The Freedom of a Christian* circulated with both prefaces.[5] At nearly the same time and working off the same outline (so that many sections of the German and Latin correspond closely but were never quite word-for-word translations of each other), Luther then completed the Latin version, adding an introduction and a lengthy appendix not found in the German. The differences between the two tracts also arose in part out of the slightly different audiences for them: the one addressed to theologians, clerics, and church leaders (for whom Latin was the common language), and one addressed to the German-speaking public, which included the nobility, townsfolk, many from the lesser clergy, and others who could read (or have Luther's writings read to them).

## Printing History

*The Freedom of a Christian* was a bestseller. Including the original Latin and German versions published in Wittenberg, there were between 1520 and 1526 thirty printings: nineteen in German, one in the dialect of the German lowlands, and eight in Latin, along with translations of the Latin into German (!) and English. It now appears that Luther sent a corrected copy to a cathedral canon in Augsburg, who forwarded it to Beatus Rhenanus, a famous humanist and early supporter in Basel (Switzerland), who added his own marginal headings and sent it on to the printer Adam Petri in Basel. The latter corrected typographical errors and probably in March 1521, published this corrected version in time for the Frankfurt book fair, titling it *A Discourse on Christian Freedom Revised by the Author*.[6] Later in the same year, Melchior Lotter reprinted this version, simply noting that it was "revised in Wittenberg." With the few exceptions mentioned in the footnotes, all of the subheadings used in the following translation have been taken from Petri's edition[a]

## The Letter to Leo X

The letter to Leo has all of the characteristics of polished Renaissance Latin prose expected for a writing that addresses the pope. Not only is the Latin itself among Luther's best writings, but the letter's argument also bears the marks of typical Latin style. Thus, Luther prosecutes two separate arguments, according to the painstaking analysis of the German linguist Birgit Stolt.[b] Her analysis is reflected in the headings of this translation. The Renaissance context of this letter, like that to Archbishop Albrecht von Brandenburg of Mainz (1490–1545), helps explain the tone of the

**6.** Rhenanus (1485–1547) was an important humanist who worked from 1511 to 1526 in Basel at the famous Froben press and was favorable toward Luther's work. (In January 1520, Martin Bucer sent him a copy of Luther's commentary on Galatians.) Philipp Melanchthon was also a great supporter of the tract. His letter from April 1521 to an unknown recipient in Schaffhausen reflects many of the themes of *The Freedom of a Christian* and even refers his correspondent to it. See *Melanchthons Briefwechsel*, vol. T1: *Texte 1–254 (1514–1522)*, ed. Richard Wetzel (Stuttgart-Bad Cannstatt: Frommann-Holzboog, 1991), 276–78 (no. 137). Wetzel notes that in 1524 this letter was included with a Nuremberg printing of *The Freedom of a Christian*.

a    See WA 7:40, "E": *Epistola Lutheriana ad Leonem Decimum summum pontificem. Liber de Christiana libertate, continens summam Christianae doctrinae, quo ad formandam mentem, & ad intelligendam Euangelii vim, nihil absolutius, nihil conducibilius neque a veteribus neque a recentioribus scriptoribus perditum est. Tu Christianae lector, relege iterum atque iterum, & Christum imbibe. Recognitus Wittembergae* (Wittenberg: Melchior Lotter, 1521). English: *A Lutheran Letter to Pope Leo X. A Book on Christian Freedom, Containing the Sum of Christian Teaching, Concerning Which Nothing More Absolute or More in Line with Either Ancient or More Recent Writers Has Been Produced for Forming the Mind and for Understanding the Power of the Gospel. You, Christian Reader, Reread This Again and Again and Drink in Christ. Reedited in Wittenberg.* For the publication, authorships, and dating of these printings, see James Hirstein's article in *Revue d'histoire et de philosophie religieuses* (forthcoming).

b    Birgit Stolt, *Studien zu Luthers Freiheitstraktat mit besonderer Rücksicht auf das Verhältnis der lateinischen und der deutschen Fassung zu einander und die Stilmittel der Rhetorik* (Stockholm: Almzvist & Wiksell, 1969).

piece—what to modern ears might appear stilted and even obsequious at times. *Not* to have addressed the pontiff with such respect would itself have been considered a shocking breech of etiquette and further proof of Luther's contempt for all authority in the church and government. To read this letter as if Luther were hiding his true feelings or even being deceitful imposes modern sensibilities on a very different age and with its very different expectations.

This letter also gives evidence of Luther's paradoxical view of the Christian's life as both free (in the gospel) and bound to the neighbor. To be sure, Luther was bound and determined to put to rest the (unfounded) rumor that he had attacked the pope's person. While he would insist that the papal court was to blame for the sorry state of the church in his day, he had no particular criticism of Leo X himself. Instead, he took direct aim at his bitterest opponent and one of the instigators of the papal bull of excommunication, Johann Eck (1486–1543). Thus, he expressed himself in the letter with remarkable freedom against his opponents— a freedom that arose for him from Christ himself. Luther could even call to mind the behavior of one of his favorite medieval theologians, Bernard of Clairvaux (1090–1153), who had written sternly to Pope Eugene III (1383–1447). This appeal to Leo, however, went unanswered.

### The Freedom of a Christian

As the letter to Leo already indicates, Luther was a child of the Renaissance. This meant that his Latin prose especially was carefully shaped according to the rhetorical rules and conventions of his day. In the case of *The Freedom of a Christian*, this means that the reader today can still detect the basic outline of his argument as it followed these conventions.[c] Even the marginal notes added to the second edition often identify these various parts. Based upon classical writings on rhetoric by Cicero (106–43 BCE) and Quintilian (c. 35– c. 100), late medieval rhetorical handbooks divided a speech

---

c   Ibid.

or tract into six parts: exordium, division of the tract, the exposition of the theme, confirmation or proof of the theme, an answer to objections to the theme, and a peroration.

Observing closely how Luther develops the argument in *The Freedom of a Christian* can help the reader in understanding the document. Luther begins by talking about the nature of faith, a key subject of debate in his case with Rome. Thereby, he intends to arouse his readers' interest in the subject and to present himself as a reliable witness or authority concerning faith. This constitutes a proper exordium, which Luther uses to encourage readers to see the importance of understanding faith, now defined not as a virtue but as an experience of struggle and mercy.

As the marginal gloss from the 1521 text notes, Luther then states the "themes" (*themata*) of his writing about Christian freedom and servitude. Yet, according to late medieval rules of rhetoric, these "themes" are not, as modern readers might think, outlining the subject of his essay (which was faith), but instead announce the proper division of the overall argument into two nearly equal sections, the first on the freedom of a Christian and the second on a Christian's servitude. It is first in the brief exposition of the themes, the so-called *narratio* following the themes' statement, that the reader discovers Luther's actual subject: *not* to divide freedom and servitude but to explain how, given their relation to faith and their use by the Apostle Paul, they cohere.

The body of the first part, or "theme," of the work consists in the *confirmatio* where Luther attempts to prove his claim that freedom and servitude cohere in the Christian life. Luther insists that the whole human being may be viewed as both inner and outer and that not works but only God's word received in faith constitutes true Christian freedom. From this premise, Luther then introduces three benefits or fruits of faith, concentrating most of his efforts on the third fruit: the marriage of the soul and Christ by faith alone. With this "joyous exchange" (as he calls it in the German version) between human sin and Christ's righteousness, the believing person receives, in addition, Christ's priesthood and kingship. Yet, by priesthood Luther does not mean having an office in the church but, rather, praying and proclaiming Christ's love; and by kingship Luther is not talking about power but the spiritual kingship of peace. Christian freedom then consists precisely in these gifts, fruits, and benefits of faith, so that Christians are lords over sin, death, the devil, and anything else that threatens them.

When Luther arrives at what he calls the second theme, that Christians are servants of all, he introduces it not as a separate theme at all but, rather, again following the rules of rhetoric, as an answer to the chief objections to the first section and its description of law and gospel, faith and its blessings. This standard component of good rhetoric since the time of Cicero, called the *confutatio*, anticipated opponents' arguments aimed at refuting the main point of a speech or writing. Here, the chief objection takes the form of derision. Opponents who were convinced that Luther's teaching on faith would lead to lawlessness and disorder, giving believers license to sin, had made exaggerated claims to that effect. Luther rebukes them ("Not so, you wicked people") and answers their objections using a series of examples from Scripture and experience that show how faith freely produces good works and, hence, serves the neighbor.[7] Throughout this section of the tract, however, Luther also restates his basic point that Christian faith does not depend upon works but only on God's mercy. Running throughout this section is a criticism of Aristotelian ethics, which dominated late medieval thinking, that a person becomes virtuous (or righteous) by doing virtuous acts. Luther argues the opposite, namely that only the one declared righteous by Christ through faith alone can bear fruit of righteousness.

The close of any proper speech or writing was the peroration, which consisted either of a summary conclusion to the argument or an appeal to the reader or listener. Indeed, Luther even signals this transition with the words, "We conclude."[8] In this case, Luther concludes that Christians live in Christ through faith and their neighbors through love. After his final "Amen," however, Luther adds a lengthy appendix that answers another misunderstanding of his argument by

**7.** See below, p. 510.

**8.** See below, p. 530.

ceremonialists, namely, that he really is supporting license and an abandonment of all good order among Christians.

His refusal to equate reform with abandoning past practices while still rebuking ceremonialists, coupled with his concern for the weak in faith, led Luther in 1522, upon returning from protective custody in the Wartburg Castle, to put the brakes on the reform movement that had arisen during his absence from Wittenberg—not on the basis of objections to the practices favored by these reform-minded colleagues (including not only Andreas Bodenstein from Karlstadt [1486–1541] but also Philip Melanchthon and Nicholas von Amsdorf [1483–1565], among others) but because such changes in practice would upset the faith of weak Christians who would not understand why they were taking place.[9] This reticence about changing forms of worship—foreign to his Roman opponents and to other leaders of reform (for example, Ulrich Zwingli [1484–1531] in Zurich and early Anabaptists)—stands as a unique mark of Wittenberg's brand of theology and may be traced to Luther's comments in *The Freedom of a Christian*.

9. See Martin Luther, *Invocavit Sermons* (March 1522), in LW 51:67–100.

**10.** The present translation is a revision of *Martin Luther, Freedom of a Christian: Luther Study Edition*, trans. Mark Tranvik (Minneapolis: Fortress Press, 2008), itself a revision of the version in LW 31:327–77, first translated by W. A. Lambert and revised by Harold J. Grimm. The present revision is based primarily upon WA 7:39–73, but also using the more recent version with extensive notes, ed. Hans-Ulrich Delius, in MLStA 2:260–309. The headings, except where noted, are translated from the second Adam Petri edition, printed in Basel in 1521.

**11.** **EXORDIUM**

**12.** Referring to the pope's ecclesiastical jurisdiction in Rome.

**13.** Luther addresses here an important part of his case with Rome. In 1518, after Pope Leo X had reaffirmed his predecessors' statements about indulgences, Luther made a formal appeal to a general council. Especially to those theologians who championed papal authority over that of a church council, this was prima facie evidence of Luther's heresy, as decrees of Pius III (1439–1503) and Julius II (1443–1513) stated. By laying the blame on the pope's advisers and Leo's generally despised predecessors, Luther sought to defend his action. (This appeal remained an important part of the Evangelical struggle with Rome throughout Luther's lifetime and is reflected in the prefaces to the *Augsburg Confession* and Luther's own *Smalcald Articles*.)

# LUTHER'S EPISTLE TO LEO X, SUPREME PONTIFF [10, d]

JESUS.[e]

MARTIN LUTHER sends greetings to Leo X, Roman Pontiff, in Christ Jesus our Lord. Amen.

[11, f]Surrounded by the monsters of this age, with which I have struggled and battled for three years, I am compelled at times to look to you and to think of you, Leo, most blessed father. Indeed, since you are widely held to be the sole cause of my battles, I cannot but think of you. And although the godless flatterers around you, who rage against me without cause, forced me to appeal from your see[12] to a future Council (given that I have no respect for the completely vain decrees of your predecessors, Pius and Julius, who with foolish tyranny prohibited such appeals),[13] nevertheless, throughout this time I have never turned my soul away from Your Holiness so as neither to desire with all my powers the very best for you and for your see nor, as far as was in me, to

---

d  Using marginal notes found in WA 7:40, "D": *Epistola Lutheriana ad Leonem Decimum summum pontificem. Dissertatis de libertate Christiana per autorem recognita Wittembergae* (Basel: Adam Petri, 1521). See the Introduction above.

e  See above, p. 264, n. 11.

f  Throughout this letter, marginal notes on the letter's structure follow the structural analysis made by Stolt.

seek the same with earnest and heartfelt prayers to God.[14] I nearly started to despise and declare victory over those who up to now have tried to frighten me with the majesty of your authority and name, except I see that there remains one thing which I cannot despise and which has been the reason for my writing to Your Holiness for a second time.[g] That is, I realize that I am accused of impertinence, now twisted into my greatest vice,[15] because I am judged to have attacked your person.[16]

# [Part One: Luther's Defense]

[17]However, so that I may confess this matter openly,[18] whenever your person has been mentioned, I am aware of having only said the greatest and best things. But if I had done otherwise, I could under no circumstances condone it; I would vote in favor of their judgment against me every time, and I would recant nothing more freely than this my impertinence and godlessness. I have called you a Daniel in Babylon, and every one of my readers knows fully well how, with extraordinary zeal, I have defended your remarkable innocence against your defiler, Sylvester [Prierias].[19] Your reputation and the fame of your blameless life, chanted in the writings of so many men the world over, are too well known and dignified to be possibly assailed in any way by anyone, no matter how great. Nor am I so foolish to attack someone whom absolutely everyone praises. As a matter of fact, I have even tried and will always try not to attack even those whom public opinion dishonors. For I take pleasure in no one's faults, since I myself am conscious enough of the log in my own eye.[h] Nor do I want to be the first who throws a stone at the adulteress.[i]

**14.** The heightened rhetoric here and throughout this letter, addressed to a Renaissance pope, indicates the care with which Luther wrote it. None of the headings in this letter come from the original.

**15.** Luther's opponents often construed his highly charged language as impudence and exaggeration. Erasmus of Rotterdam (1466–1536) nicknamed him *doctor hyperbolicus*, "the exaggerating teacher."

**16.** Personal attacks of governmental or ecclesiastical rulers were viewed as especially inappropriate.

**17.**     **Answering Three Questions in His Defense**
*1. Whether He Committed the Offense*

**18.** Luther answers the charges according to the three questions of the judicial genre of speech: whether he committed the offense; what he actually did; whether he acted rightly.

**19.** Luther stated this in his 1518 tract, *Response to the Dialogue of Sylvester Prierias concerning the Power of the Pope* (WA 1:679, 5–7). Sylvester (Mazzolini) Prierias (1456–1523) was named after the city of his birth (Prierio). A Dominican (as was Johann Tetzel [1460–1519]), he strongly defended papal authority and infallibility in matters of teaching and practice. Luther viewed this as an insult to the pope because it exalted him over Christ and the Scriptures.

---

g   The first time was the preface to the *Explanations of the Ninety-Five Theses* of 1518. See WA 1:527–29.

h   Matt. 7:3.

i   John 8:1-11.

**20.** *2. What Luther Actually Did and Whether This Was Proper*

[20] Now, generally I have sharply attacked ungodly teachings, and I have been quick to snap at my opponents not because of their bad morals but because of their godlessness. I do not repent of this in the least, as I have resolved in my soul, despite the contempt of others, to persist in this fervent zeal, following the example of Christ, who in his zeal called his adversaries "a brood of vipers," "blind," "hypocrites," and "children of the devil."[j] And Paul branded the Magician [Elymas] a "son of the devil . . . full of deceit and villainy."[k] Others he ridiculed as "dogs," "deceivers," and "adulterators."[l] If you consider any sensitive audience, no one will seem more biting and unrestrained than Paul. What is more biting than the prophets? The mad multitude of flatterers imitates the ever so sensitive ears of our rational age, so that, as soon as we sense disapproval of our ideas, we cry that we are bitten. As long as we can rebuff the truth by labeling it something else, we flee from it under the pretext of its being snappish, impatient, and unrestrained. What good is salt if it has lost its bite?[m] What use is the edge of a sword if it does not cut? "Accursed is the one who does the Lord's work deceitfully."[n]

**21.** *3. Summary Conclusion*

[21] For this reason, most excellent Leo, I beg you to admit that this letter vindicates me. And I beg you to convince yourself that I have never thought ill of your person and, moreover, that I am the kind of person who eternally wishes the very best things happen to you and that for me this strife is not with any person over morals but over the Word of truth alone. In everything else I will yield to anyone. I cannot and

---

*j* See Matt. 23:33, 13, 17; and John 8:44, respectively.

*k* Acts 13:10.

*l* Phil. 3:2; 2 Cor. 11:13; 2:17 (following the Latin; NRSV: "peddlers").

*m* Classical Latin authors often compared salt (especial "black salt") with sharpness (e.g., Pliny [the Elder] (23-79), *Historia naturalis*, 10, 72, 93, par. 198) and sarcasm (e.g., Catullus [c. 84-54 BCE], 13, 5). See also Matt. 5:13.

*n* Jer. 48:10 (Vulgate).

will not yield or deny the Word. If a person has thought something else about me or otherwise interpreted my positions, then that one is not thinking straight nor interpreting my true positions.

[22] However, I have rightly cursed your see, called the Roman Curia,[23] which neither you nor any human being can deny is more corrupt than Babylon or Sodom[24] and, as far as I can tell, is composed of depraved, desperate, and notorious godlessness. And I have made known that, under your name and under the cover of the Roman Church, the people of Christ are being undeservedly deceived. Indeed, I have thus resisted and will continue to resist [the Curia], as long as the Spirit of faith lives in me—not that I would strive for the impossible or that I would hope that, given the furious opposition of so many flatterers, my works alone would improve anything in that chaotic Babylon, but I do acknowledge the debt owed to my fellow Christians,[o] whom I must warn so that fewer may perish or at least have milder symptoms from that Roman plague. Indeed, as you yourself know, for many years nothing else has been flooding the world from Rome than the devastation of possessions, bodies, and souls, and the worst examples of the worst possible things. All this is clearer than day to everyone. Moreover, out of the Roman Church, once the holiest of all, has been fashioned a completely licentious den of thieves, the most shameless of all brothels, the kingdom of sin, death, and hell, so that were the Antichrist to come, he could hardly think of anything that would add to its wickedness.[25]

**22.** **Proof That Luther Acted Properly**
*1. The Corruption in the Roman Curia*

**23.** The papal court (Latin: *curia*), consisting of cardinals, bishops, and other clerical functionaries.

**24.** Rev. 18:2-24 and 11:8, respectively names for the powers opposed to Christ and Christians during the end times.

**25.** Faced with what he perceived as the Roman Curia's intransigence, Luther moved from granting the papacy human authority over the churches to condemning it (but not individual bishops of Rome) as in league with or identified with the Antichrist. By the late Middle Ages, many Christian thinkers assumed that at the world's end an Antichrist would arise to do battle with God's elect.

o   Literally, "brothers."

**26.** *2. Luther's Compassion for the Pope*

**27.** An attempt to poison Leo X had indeed been made in 1517.

**28.** Luther was quoting Baptista Mantuanus (1447–1516), *Varia ad Falconem Sinibaldum epigrammata,* a collection of epigrams against corruption in Rome. Luther also quoted this text in *On the Bondage of the Will* (LW 33:53) and used Mantuanus's work in his 1545 tract *Against the Roman Papacy: An Institution of the Devil* (LW 41:257–376). Gout was considered an incurable disease.

**29.**      *3. What the Pope Should Do*

**30.** He was a member of the powerful de Medicis. From this point on, Luther uses the word *gloria* (glory or fame or boasting) to describe the situation in Rome and with his enemies.

[26] In the meantime, you, Leo, sit as a lamb in the midst of wolves, as Daniel in the midst of lions, and you dwell with Ezekiel among the scorpions.[p] How can you alone oppose these monsters? Add three or four of your best and most learned cardinals! "What are they among so many?"[q] Before you had even begun setting up the remedy, you would have all been poisoned to death.[27] It is all over for the Roman Curia. The wrath of God has fallen upon it completely. It hates councils; it fears being reformed; it cannot allay its raging godlessness; and it fulfills the eulogy written for its "mother," about whom is said, "We tried to heal Babylon, but she has not been healed. Let us forsake her."[r] To be sure, it was part of your office and that of your cardinals to heal these ills, but "this gout derided the physician's hands,"[28] and neither horse "nor chariot responds to the reins."[s] Touched by deep affection, I have always been grieved, most excellent Leo, that you, who were worthy of far better times, became pope in this day and age. For the Roman Curia is not worthy of you or people like you but only Satan himself, who now actually rules in that Babylon more than you do.

[29] O that, having cast aside the glory that your completely accursed enemies heap upon you, you would instead live on the small income of a parish priest or on your family's inheritance.[30] Only the Iscariots, sons of perdition,[t] are worthy of glorying in this kind of glory. For what are you accomplishing in the Curia, my Leo, except that the more wicked and accursed a person is, the more happily such a one uses your name and authority to destroy the wealth and souls of human beings, to increase wickedness, and to suppress faith and truth throughout the church of God? O truly most unhappy Leo, sitting on that most dangerous throne—I am telling you the truth, because I wish you well! For if Bernard

*p*    Matt. 10:16; Dan. 6:16; and Ezek. 2:6, respectively.

*q*    See John 6:9.

*r*    Jer. 51:9 (Vulgate).

*s*    Virgil (70–19 BCE), *Georgics,* 1, 514.

*t*    The family of Judas Iscariot, as he was labeled in John 17:12.

had compassion on Pope Eugenius,[31] when the Holy See—although already then very corrupt—still governed with more hope [for improvement], why should we not complain about the three hundred years of corruption and ruin that has been added since then? Is it not true that under the great expanse of heaven nothing is more corrupt, pestilential, and despicable than the Roman Curia? For it even surpasses by any measure the godlessness of the Turks, so that, truth be told, what was once the gate of heaven is now the very gaping mouth of hell—such a mouth that because of the wrath of God cannot be blocked. This leaves only one option in these

31. Bernard of Clairvaux, a Cistercian monk, wrote *On Consideration* (MPL 182:727–808), addressing it to Pope Eugene III (d. 1153) and warning about the dangers connected to the papal office.

486     *The Glory of their Times, or*

*An. Chrifti*
*1130.*
*Sanctus*
*Bernardus.*

*S. BERNARDVS.*

IT is not fitting that this great Light which God did set up should be hid under a bushell, but that his pietie and vertues should be celebrated to all posteritie : Hee was borne in those parts of *Burgundie,* in which his Father held much land and large possessions. His parents were noble and religious. His Fathers name was *Tecelinus,* a great Souldier, and such a one as Saint *Iohn* wish'd others to be, *laid violent hands on none;* but kept himselfe within the bounds of civility and sobriety, and so followed his Commanders here, that hee did not neglect his chiefe Commander in Heaven: his mothers name was *Aleth,*
sprung

A seventeenth-century depiction of Bernard of Clairvaux (1090–1153), Cistercian monk and theologian.

**32.**     *4. Recapitulation of Part One*

miseries: perhaps we can call back and rescue a few from this Roman abyss (as I said)."

[32] Observe, my father Leo, my reason and design for raving against that pestilential see. For I completely avoided raging against your person because I even hoped that I would gain your favor and cause your rescue—if I could have quickly and decisively broken open that prison of yours or, rather, your hell. For it would have been useful for your sake and your rescue, along with that of many others, had an attack by all talented, able people been able to mitigate some of the confusion in that godless Curia. Those who harm the Curia serve your office; those who by any and all means curse it glorify Christ. In short, Christians are those who are not "Romans."

## [Part Two: A Narrative of Luther's Case]

**33.**     *1. The Real Cause of the Dispute*

**34.** Luther considered his unguarded remarks at the Leipzig Debate were the real cause of the problem and demanded explanation for a successful defense of his case before Leo. He returns to the debate in the next section when describing events chronologically.

[33] But, to enlarge upon this, attacking the Roman Curia or raising questions about it had never crossed my mind at all. [34] For seeing that all remedies for saving it had failed, I had only contempt for it, served it divorce papers,[v] and said to it, "Let the evildoer still do evil, and the filthy still be filthy."[w] I devoted my time to the peaceful and quiet studies of Holy Scripture, by which I wanted to assist my brothers around me. When I made some progress in this, Satan opened his

---

*u*   See above, p. 475.

*v*   See Jer. 3:8.

*w*   Rev. 22:11.

eyes and goaded his servant Johann Eck,[35] a noted enemy of Christ, with an uncontrollable desire for glory. This resulted in Eck dragging me into an unexpected arena for combat and trapping me on one little word that in passing I let slip concerning the primacy of the Roman Church.[36] This glorious "Thraso,"[37] foaming at the mouth and gnashing his teeth, boasted that he would risk everything "for the glory of God" and "for the honor of the Holy Apostolic See." Puffed up with the prospect of abusing your power for himself, he expected nothing but certain victory, seeking not so much the primacy of Peter as his own preeminence among the theologians of this age. To achieve that goal, he imagined no small advantage in triumphing over Luther. When [the debate] ended unhappily for the Sophist,[38] an incredible madness seized the man, for he sensed that whatever of the Roman shame had come to light through me was his fault alone.[39]

**35.** Johann Eck, professor of theology at the University of Ingolstadt, opposed Luther already in 1518 and challenged Luther's colleague Andreas Bodenstein from Karlstadt to a debate in Leipzig, to which Luther then was added as an opponent. It took place in June 1519. See LW 31:307–25 for some of the 1519 documents from the proceedings.

**36.** Luther admitted in a publication leading up to the debate that the papacy of the last four hundred years was in error (proposition 13 in LW 31:318). At the debate, he admitted that councils could also err. Luther's intentions seemed more focused than he was admitting to Leo.

**37.** A vain character in the Roman author Terence's (d. 159 BCE) comedy *The Eunuch*, known for rhetorical bombast.

**38.** In the Renaissance, the label "sophist" implied someone who could nitpick about logic while missing the point of an argument. The universities established to judge the debate found in Eck's favor, but Luther won in the court of public opinion through the early publication of several accounts favorable to him.

**39.** After the Leipzig Debates, Eck made several trips to Rome to secure Luther's condemnation as a heretic. He also constantly wrote against Luther and his Wittenberg colleagues throughout his life.

**40.**     *2. The Progression of the Case*

**41.** Luther had to prove that he had done everything in his power to avoid this conflict.

**42.** Cardinal Cajetan (Tommaso de Vio), was also known by the name of St. Sisto's in Rome, where he was cardinal presbyter. As part of the Dominican order, he was a famous Renaissance interpreter of Thomas Aquinas (1225–1274). He was papal legate (ambassador) to the 1518 imperial Diet of Augsburg.

**43.** See Luther's *Proceedings at Augsburg*, above, pp 121–65. Although Luther describes Cajetan's behavior as overstepping his mandate as legate, Cajetan only may have violated the specific agreement with the Elector of Saxony, Luther's prince.

**44.** Karl von Miltitz was the papal ambassador north of the Alps in 1518 and 1519 with instructions to resolve the dispute with Luther.

**45.** Luther's own prince and the patron of the University of Wittenberg.

**46.** At the 1521 Diet of Worms, in addition to his public appearance before the diet, Luther met at several points with the archbishop of Trier, Richard von Greiffenklau zu Vollrads (1467–1531).

[40] Therefore, most excellent Leo, allow me this once to make my case[41] here and to accuse your true enemies. I believe you are aware what your legate, Cardinal St. Sisto,[42] an unwise and unfortunate—indeed, untrustworthy—person, had wanted [to do] with me. When out of reverence for your name I placed myself and the entire affair into his hands, he did not attempt to establish peace—which he could easily have done with one simple word, since at the time I had promised to be silent and make an end to my case if he commanded my adversaries to do likewise. Instead, as a man seeking glory, he was not content with this agreement and instead began to defend my adversaries, to allow them freedom [of speech] and to command me to recant, even though this was not part of his mandate at all.[43] So, just when the case was in a very favorable place [for resolution], he came with his ill-natured tyranny and made it much worse. Thus, the blame for whatever followed this was not Luther's but totally Cajetan's, who did not permit me to remain silent and quiet as I at the time had requested with all my might. What more could I have possibly done?

Next followed Karl Miltitz, also a nuncio of Your Holiness.[44] He traveled back and forth in various negotiations, omitting nothing in regards to restoring the case's status quo, which Cajetan had rashly and arrogantly upset. Finally, with great difficulty but assisted by the Most Illustrious Prince, Elector Frederick,[45] he managed to speak with me several times privately, where once again I yielded to your authority and was prepared to keep silent, even accepting as a judge [in the case] either the Archbishop of Trier or the Bishop of Naumburg.[46] And thus it was settled and so ordered. While these good things were occurring and held the prospect [for success], behold, your other great enemy Eck[x] madly rushed in with the Leipzig disputation, which he set up with Dr. Karlstadt. And when a new question arose concerning the primacy of the pope, he turned

---

x    Luther is making a play on words: "Ecce . . . Eck" (Behold . . . Eck).

his concealed weapons on me and thoroughly destroyed the plans for peace. In the meantime, Karl Miltitz waited. The disputation was held, judges were chosen, and yet no decision was reached. Small wonder, given Eck's lies, deceptions, and trickery, that everything everywhere was so completely stirred up, aggravated, and confused that, whatever the outcome of the decision, a greater conflagration would have flared up. For he sought glory not truth. Here, too, I left nothing undone that I should have carried out.

I concede that on this occasion much of Roman corruption came to light. But in this matter, whatever wrong was committed was Eck's fault. He took on a task beyond his abilities. While striving furiously for his own glory, he revealed the shame of Rome to the whole world. This one is your enemy, my Leo, or rather, the enemy of your Curia. We can learn from his example that no enemy is more pernicious than a flatterer.[y] For what did his flattery accomplish other than a kind of evil that not a single king would have been able to accomplish? For today the name "Roman Curia" reeks the world over, and papal authority languishes. Its notorious ignorance is now despised.[z] We would have heard nothing of this had Eck not upset the peace agreement between Karl and me. He himself senses this plainly and, too late and to no avail, is offended by the subsequent publication of my books. He should have thought of this earlier, when, just like a bleating goat, he madly raved about his own glory and sought nothing but his own advantage with you—at your great peril. That completely vain man hoped that I would stop and be silent out of fear for your name, since I do not believe that he supposed his own intelligence and learning would be enough. Now, because he realizes that I have confidence and continue to speak out, he understands albeit with overdue sorrow for his rash behavior—if he understands at

The coat of arms of
Thomas Cardinal Cajetan,
also called Tommaso de Vio.

---

y    See Cicero, *De Amicitia*, 91 (25).

z    See, e.g., the reference to "Roman ignorance" in Maurus Servius Honoratus (4th–5th century), *Commentary on the Aeneid of Virgil*, 8, 597.

all—that there is One in heaven who "resists the proud" and humbles the presumptuous.[a]

Therefore, after we had accomplished nothing by this disputation [in Leipzig] except greater confusion about the case in Rome, Karl von Miltitz came a third time, this time to the [Augustinian] fathers gathered for the chapter meeting of their order.[47] He asked their advice about how to resolve the case, which was now greatly disturbing and dangerous. Since there was no hope of proceeding against me by force (thanks to God's mercy!), some of their leaders were sent here to me. They requested that at least I show honor to the person of your Blessedness and in a humble letter plead that you and I are innocent. [They thought] that this matter was not yet completely hopeless as long as Leo X out of his innate goodness took a hand in it. Now, I have always offered and desired to keep the peace so that I might devote myself to quieter and more useful studies, since I have raged in this matter with such spirit in order that, by using great and forceful words and animus, I could restrain those whom I viewed as being no match for me at all. In this situation then, I not only freely yielded [to the delegation] but also accepted [the proposal] with joy and gratitude as a most welcomed kindness, provided that our hope could be realized.

[48] So, most Holy Father, I come and, even now, prostrate myself before you, begging, if possible, that you lay your hands on those flatterers and enemies of peace (who only pretend to want peace) and rein them in. In turn, let no one presume, Most Holy Father, that I will recant, unless such a person wants to envelop this case in even greater turmoil. Furthermore, I will permit no binding laws for interpreting the Word of God, since "the Word of God must not be bound" because it teaches freedom in all other matters.[b] Save for these two things, there is nothing that I could not or would not freely do or endure. I hate contentions. I will

---

**47.** This meeting of the heads of the German friaries of the Augustinian order met under the retiring vicar general, Johann von Staupitz (c. 1460–1524), in Eisleben on 28 August 1520, where von Miltitz also appeared. They sent a delegation to Wittenberg in early September. It consisted of von Staupitz, the new vicar general Wenceslaus Linck (1482–1547), and others.

**48.**     *3. A Closing Plea for Mercy*

---

a   See, e.g., 1 Pet. 5:5 and James 4:6.

b   2 Tim. 2:9, an indirect reference to the tract, *The Freedom of a Christian*, to which this letter became attached.

not provoke anyone at all. But, at the same time, I do not want to be provoked. But if I am provoked (with Christ as my teacher), I will not be at a loss for words. For, once this controversy has been brought before you and settled, Your Holiness could, with a short and simple word, command both parties to be silent and keep the peace, which is what I have always wanted to hear.

## [Peroration: Advice for Pope Leo]

Consequently, My Father Leo, avoid listening to those sirens who turn you from being purely a human being into a demi-god in order that you can command and decide whatever you wish. Do not let this happen; nor will you prevail in this way! You are a servant of servants and, more than all other human beings, in a most miserable and dangerous position. Do not let those deceive you who imagine that you are the lord of the world, who allow no one to be Christian outside of your authority and who babble on that you have power over heaven, hell, and purgatory.[49] They are your enemies and seek to destroy your soul, as Isaiah says, "O my people, those who call you blessed deceive you."[c] Those who place you above a council and the universal church err. Those who attribute to you alone the right to interpret Scripture err. For they seek to establish all manner of ungodliness in the Church under your name, and, alas, through them Satan has made great inroads among your predecessors.[d] In sum, believe none of those who exalt you but only those who humble you. For this is the judgment of God, who "has brought down the powerful from their thrones and lifted up the lowly."[e] Look at how different Christ is from his successors, although they still all want to be his vicars.[50] And I fear that most of them have been too literally his "vicars." For a person is a vicar only in the absence of a superior. But if the

**49.** Part of the original claims in the *95 Theses*. See above, pp. 35–37.

**50.** This technical term designates the pope as a substitute (vicarious) ruler of the church in Christ's visible absence.

c    Isa. 3:12 (Vulgate).

d    See Luther's *Address to the Christian Nobility* (1520), above, pp. 387–89.

e    Luke 1:52.

pope rules when Christ is absent and not present and dwelling in his heart, what is that but to be a Vicar of Christ? And then, what is the church other than a whole group of people without Christ? Truly, what is such a vicar except an Antichrist and idol? How much more correctly did the apostles call themselves servants of a present Christ than vicars of an absent Christ!

Perhaps I am presumptuous in attempting to teach such an exalted person, from whom all ought to be taught and (as your "plagues" boast)[51] from whom "the thrones of those who judge"[52] receive the [final] decree. But I emulate Saint Bernard in his book *On Consideration*, addressed to Pope Eugenius, which every pope should commit to memory.[f] I do this not from a desire to instruct you but from a sense of duty arising from pure and faithful solicitude that compels us to respect only the complete safety of our neighbors and that does not allow any consideration of their worthiness or unworthiness—being focused only on their dangers and particular situations. For since I know that Your Holiness is twisted and tossed about in Rome—that is, driven by unending dangers and surrounded by the highest seas—and that you are laboring on these things in miserable conditions such that you stand in need of even the smallest help from the least of the brothers, it did not seem foolish to me if for the moment I would forget your high majesty while fulfilling the duty of love. I do not want to flatter you in such a serious and dangerous situation. As far as that goes, if I am not understood to be your friend and most obedient servant, there is One who understands and judges.

### [Introduction to the Tract][53]

In conclusion, so that I might not approach you, Holy Father, empty-handed, I offer this little tract, published under your name, in the prospect of an established peace and good hope. In it you can get a taste of the kinds of studies with

51. Luther's description of the pope's flatterers. See above, p. 477.

52. That is, the bishops.

53. Renaissance dedications typically ended with a brief description of the book to which they were attached.

f   See above, p. 479.

which I could and would occupy myself far more fruitfully, if only your godless flatterers permitted it now and before. It is a small thing with respect to its size, but (unless I am mistaken) it contains a summary of the whole Christian life, if you understand its meaning. Poor man that I am, I have nothing else to present to you. But then you do not need to be enriched by any other gift save a spiritual one. Therefore, I commend myself to your fatherly goodness. May the Lord Jesus preserve you forever! Amen.

Wittenberg, September 6, 1520.

# ON CHRISTIAN FREEDOM

## Introduction[g]

Many people view Christian faith as something easy, and quite a few people even count it as if it were related to the virtues.[54] They do this because they have not judged faith in light of any experience, nor have they ever tasted its great power.[h]

### [Faith Is Learned through Tribulations][i]

This is because a person who has not tasted its spirit in the midst of trials and misfortune cannot possibly write well about faith or understand what has been written about it. But one who has had even a small taste of faith can never write, speak, reflect, or hear enough about it. As Christ says in John 4[:14], it is a "spring of water welling up to eternal life."

g  This subhead is not in sixteenth-century editions of the tract.
h  The same Latin word is translated here "virtues" or "power."
i  With few exceptions recorded in footnotes, all subtitles come from the second edition of the tract, printed in Basel by Adam Petri in 1521. See the introductory material, p. 468f, above.

54. In medieval moral theology, faith, hope, and love were the chief theological virtues (based on 1 Cor. 13:13). Over against this prevailing view, Luther understood faith relationally (experientially) as confidence or trust, arising in the midst of trials. He distinguished it from mere intellectual assent to doctrinal truths and thus opposed medieval theology, which derived its definition of faith from the basic Aristotelian distinction between "matter" and "form," interpreting the Latin version of Gal. 5:6 as "faith *formed* by love," meaning that faith by itself was insufficient (only the "material principle" of a saving disposition toward God), completed only by the "formal principle" of love for God.

Although I cannot boast of my own abundance of faith and I also know quite well how short my own supply is, nevertheless—given that I have been troubled by great and various trials[55]—I hope I can attain to at least a drop of faith. And I hope that I can talk about faith in a way that, if not more elegant, is certainly clearer than has been done in the past by the fancy writers and the subtle disputants alike, who have not even understood their own writings.[56]

### The Main Themes [j]

In order to point out an easier way for common folk[k] (for I serve only them), I am proposing two themes[57] concerning the freedom and servitude of the spirit.

The Christian individual[l] is a completely free lord of all, subject to none.

The Christian individual is a completely dutiful servant[m] of all, subject to all.

Although these topics appear to contradict one another, nevertheless, if they can be found to be in agreement, they will serve our purposes beautifully. For both are from the Apostle Paul, when he says in 1 Cor. 9[:19], "For though I am free with respect to all, I have made myself a slave to all" and in Rom. 13[:8], "Owe nothing to anyone except to love one another." But "love" by its very nature is dutiful and serves the one who is loved. The same was true of Christ who,

55. For Luther, trials (*tentationes*; often denoted by the German word *Anfechtungen*, attacks or struggles) marked the Christian life of faith from beginning to end. Thus, Luther is not simply referring here to earlier struggles as an Augustinian friar concerned with God's righteousness and penitence but to his entire life as a believer. For an even earlier reflection on this notion, see his *Explanations of the Ninety-Five Theses*, thesis 15 (LW 31:125–30, esp. 129).

56. Luther probably had in mind both "fancy" humanist writers, such as Erasmus (in his *Handbook of the Christian Soldier*), and Scholastic theologians known for disputations, such as Gabriel Biel.

57. These two statements provide the basic themes of the entire tract, explicated below beginning on pp. 489 and 510, respectively.

j　The word "themes" (*themata*) is a Greek loan word and a technical term in rhetoric and dialectics for the main topic or central proposition of a speech or an argument.

k　Latin: *rudes*. This term can mean unlettered or uncultivated but here means the simple or common people, unfamiliar with the complexities of Scholastic theology. It is at this point that the German version begins. For further references to Luther's orientation toward the commoner, see his *Treatise on Good Works*, above, pp. 265f.

l　Latin here and in the next line: *Christianus homo*.

m　*Servus* can be translated either servant or slave but here is rendered servant to correspond with Luther's German version (*Knecht*). In the Pauline letters, the NRSV translates the Greek *doulos* as "slave").

although Lord of all, was nevertheless "born of a woman, born under the law"[n] and who was at the same time free and slave, that is, at the same time "in the form of God" and "in the form of a slave."[58, o]

Let us approach these two themes from a rather distant and unsophisticated starting point.[p] Every human being consists of two natures: a spiritual and a bodily one. According to the spiritual nature, which people label the soul, the human being is called a spiritual, inner, and new creature. According to the bodily nature, which people label the flesh, a human being is called the fleshly, outer, and old creature.[59] Paul writes about this in 2 Cor. 4[:16], "Even though our outer nature is wasting away, our inner nature is being renewed day by day." This distinction results in the fact that in the Scripture these contrary things are said about the same person, because these two "human beings" fight against each other in the very same human being, as in Gal. 5[:17], "For what the flesh desires is opposed to the spirit, and what the spirit desires is opposed to the flesh."[q]

## [The Spiritual, New, and Inner Person][60, r]

In looking at the inner person first, we grasp how someone may become righteous,[s] free, and truly Christian, that is, "a spiritual, new, and inner person."[t]

**58.** The basic themes of this tract first arose in Luther's *Two Kinds of Righteousness* from 1519 (LW 31:297–306, esp. 297), itself perhaps derived from a sermon on the appointed epistle lesson for Palm Sunday, Phil. 2:6-11.

**59.** By defining the whole human being according to these two aspects or natures, Luther is not simply taking over Platonic or other philosophical divisions between material and spiritual worlds. He often equated *soul* with the biblical term *heart*.

**60.** This begins the first main section of the tract on the first of the two themes introduced above. The second begins on p. 510.

n   An allusion to Gal. 4:4.
o   An allusion to Phil. 2:6-7.
p   *Altior* could mean distant, deeper, or ancient. Coupled with *crassior*, it seems to indicate either an old, crude example or one that seems far removed from the two stated themes.
q   In the Greek and Latin texts of Galatians, the word "spirit" can also refer to the Holy Spirit.
r   This subtitle was not in any sixteenth-century text.
s   Except where noted, the Latin words *iustus* and *iustitia* will be translated "righteous" and "righteousness," not "justice," which in current English usage denotes conformity to a legal principle.
t   An allusion to the wording in the preceding paragraph.

## What Christian Freedom Does Not Consist In

It is evident that no external thing at all, whatever its name, has any part in producing Christian righteousness or freedom. Nor does it produce unrighteousness or servitude. This can be proven by a simple argument. How can it benefit the soul if the body is in good health—free and active, eating and drinking and doing what it pleases—when even the most ungodly slaves to complete wickedness may overflow in such things? On the other hand, how could poor health or captivity or hunger or thirst or any other external misfortune harm the soul, when even the godliest, purest, and freest consciences[61] are afflicted with such things? Not one of these things touches upon the freedom or servitude of the soul. Thus, it does not help the soul if the body wears the sacred robes set apart for priests or enters sacred places or performs sacred duties or prays, fasts, abstains from certain foods, or does absolutely any work connected with the body.[62] Righteousness and freedom of the soul will require something completely different, since the things just mentioned could easily be done by some ungodly person and since such efforts result only in producing hypocrites. On the other side, the soul is not harmed if the body wears street clothes, goes around in secular places, eats and drinks like everyone else, does not pray aloud, and fails to do all the things mentioned above that hypocrites could do.

## The Word of God Is Necessary for the Soul

Moreover, so that we may exclude everything—even contemplation, meditation, and whatever else can be done by the soul's efforts—all of this has no benefit. One thing and one thing alone is necessary for the Christian life, righteousness, and freedom, and that is the most holy word of God, the Gospel of Christ.[63] As John 11[:25] states: "I am the Resurrection and the Life, whoever believes in me will never die." And John 8[:36]: "If the Son makes you free, you will be free indeed." And Matt. 4[:4]: "One does not live by bread alone but by every word that comes from the mouth

**61.** Luther often used the term *conscience* not simply as an ethical category but to denote the entire human being standing before the righteous God, as here.

**62.** This argument implies criticism of late medieval popular piety, which assumed that pilgrimages to see relics, fasting, and sacred acts performed by priests did affect the soul's standing before God. Luther's readers might also have been familiar with even harsher criticism of the late medieval priesthood by humanists and other pamphleteers. See the "appendix" below, pp. 531–38.

**63.** For Luther, the phrase "word of God" rarely meant simply the Bible but more generally God's oral, direct proclamation. Thus, here he modifies the phrase with the words (capitalized in the original) "Gospel of Christ." The German version, also written by Luther, has: ". . . except the holy Gospel, the word of God preached by Christ." Luther understood God's word not simply as informative but as powerful and creative, present

of God." Therefore, we may consider it certain and firmly established, that the soul can lack everything except the word of God. Without it absolutely nothing else satisfies the soul. But when soul has the word, it is rich and needs nothing else, because the word of God is the word of life, truth, light, peace, righteousness, salvation, joy, freedom, wisdom, power, grace, glory, and every imaginable blessing.[64]

### David in Psalm 119 [65]

This is why the prophet throughout Psalm 119 and in so many other places [in the Psalter] yearns and sighs with groans and cries for the word of God.

### God's Cruelest Disaster

Again, there is no crueler disaster arising from God's wrath than when it sends "a famine of the hearing of his word," as stated in Amos 8[:11],[u] just as there is no greater grace than whenever God sends forth his word, as in Ps. 107[:20]. "He sent out his word and healed them and delivered them from their destruction." And Christ was not sent into the world for any other office than the word. Moreover, the apostles, bishops and the entire order of clerics[v] have been called and established only for the ministry of the word.

### What the Word of God Is

You may ask, "What is this word and how should it be used, when there are so many words of God?" I respond as follows. Paul explains what this word is in Rom. 1[:1, 3]: "The gospel of God ... concerning his Son," who was made flesh, suffered, rose, and was glorified through the Spirit, the Sanctifier.[w] Thus, to preach Christ means to feed, justify, free, and save the soul—provided a person believes the preaching. For faith

in creation (Genesis 1) and in the church's proclamation of the good news of Christ (whom John 1 calls the Word of God). Luther's insistence on the Word "alone" (*solum*) is the basis for later comments about faith alone.

**64.** Luther uses one of his favorite rhetorical devices, congeries (a heaping up of words), to emphasize the wide-ranging work of God's word.

**65.** Luther and most of his contemporaries assumed that King David, whom they often called a prophet because of the association of many psalms with Christ, wrote many if not all of the psalms. Luther wrote similar things about Psalm 119 in his 1539 preface to his German works (LW 34:279–88).

---

u  Luther's citation of Amos is a paraphrase.
v  Latin: *ordo clericorum*, that is, priests. Luther returns to this point later in the tract (p. 508f.).
w  Paraphrasing Rom. 1:3-4. "Sanctificator" here means the One who makes holy.

alone is the saving and efficacious use of the word of God. Rom. 10[:9] states: "If you confess with your heart that Jesus is Lord and believe in your heart that God raised him from the dead, you will be saved," and again [in v. 4]: "For Christ is the end of the law, so that there may be righteousness for everyone who believes." And Rom. 1[:17] states: "The one who is righteous will live by faith."

## Faith Alone Justifies

For the word of God cannot be received or honored by any works but by faith alone.[66] Therefore, it is clear that the soul needs the word alone for life and righteousness, because if the soul could be justified by anything else, it would not need the word and, consequently, would not need faith. Indeed, this faith absolutely cannot exist in connection with works, that is to say, in connection with any presumption of yours to be justified at the same time by any works whatsoever. For this would be "to limp in two different opinions" to worship Baal[x] and to "kiss [my] hand," which, as Job says, "is a great iniquity."[y]

### What Must Be Believed

Therefore, when you begin to believe,[67] you discover at the same time that everything in you is completely blameworthy, damnable sins, as Rom. 3[:23] states: "All have sinned and fall short of the glory of God." And Rom. 3[:10-12] says, "There is no one who is righteous," no one does good, "all have turned aside, altogether they have done worthless things."[z] By this knowledge you will realize that you need Christ, who suffered and rose again for you, in order that, believing in him, you may become another human being by this faith, because all your sins are forgiven and you are justified by another's merits, namely, by Christ's alone.

---

**66.** First in the spring of 1518 (e.g., in his *Sermon on Penance* [*Sermo de poenitentia*; WA 1:324, 15]), Luther used the Latin phrase "faith alone justifies" (*sola fide iustificet*) in print. By stressing faith *alone*, he rejected the common medieval stance, based upon the Aristotelian notion that because everything consisted of matter and form, faith and love together justified. (See above, p. 487, n. 54.) For Luther, faith itself was not a human work. Thus, he was also attacking the notion, championed by Gabriel Biel and other Nominalist theologians, that "to those who do what is in them God will not deny grace." This whole paragraph is only in the Latin version.

**67.** In the German version, Luther uses the phrases "to believe firmly" and "to trust." In Latin, he uses "to believe" (*credere*) and "faith" (*fides*). Already here Luther is moving from law (commands that reveal and condemn sin) to gospel (promises that provide faith in Christ), a central part of his theology. See below, p. 494.

---

x    An allusion to 1 Kgs. 18:21, Elijah's mocking of the priests of Baal.

y    Job 31:27, which contrasts worship of God to worship of gold, nature, or the self.

z    Reading with the Vulgate.

### A Human Being Is Justified by No External Work

Because this faith can only rule the inner person, as Rom. 10[:10] says ("one believes with the heart and so is justified"), and because this faith alone justifies, it is clear that the inner person cannot be justified, freed, or saved by any external work or activity at all and that no works whatever have anything to do with the inner person. In the same way, on the other hand, the inner person becomes guilty and a condemned slave of sin only by ungodliness and unbelief of the heart and not by any external sin or work. It follows that the primary concern of each and every Christian ought to be that, by putting aside the supposition about works, they strengthen faith alone more and more and through that faith "grow . . . in knowledge" not of works but "of Christ Jesus," who suffered and rose again for them, as Peter in 2 Pet. 3[:18] teaches.[a] For no other work makes a Christian. Thus, when the Jews in John 6[:28] asked what they should do to perform the works of God, Christ dismissed their multitude of works, which he realized puffed them up, and prescribed one work for them, saying, "This is the work of God, that you believe in him whom he has sent," for "it is on him that God the Father has set his seal."[b]

### Faith Is an Incomparable Treasure

Therefore, true faith in Christ is an incomparable treasure that includes with it complete salvation and protection from all evil, as it says in Mark 16[:16]: "The one who believes and is baptized will be saved; but the one who does not believe will be condemned." Isaiah contemplated this treasure and foretold it in chapter 10[:23, 22]: "The Lord will make an abbreviated and completed word upon earth," and "a

---

a   Literally: "In the last chapter of 1 Peter," leading most editors and translators to refer to 1 Peter 5:10. However, the preceding language comes from the last chapter of 2 Peter (3:18): "But grow in the grace and knowledge of our Lord and Savior Jesus Christ."

b   John 6:29, 27. See the *Treatise on Good Works*, above, p. 267.

completed abbreviation will overflow with righteousness."[c] It is as if to say, "Faith, which is a compact and complete fulfillment of the law, will fill believers with such righteousness that they will need nothing else for righteousness." So, too, Paul says in Rom. 10[:10]: "For one believes with the heart and so is justified."

## Scripture Contains Commands and Promises[d]

You may be asking, however, how it comes about that faith alone justifies and how it confers so many great treasures without works, given that so many works, ceremonies,[68] and laws are prescribed in the Scriptures. I answer this way. Before all else, remember what has been said above, namely, that faith alone without works justifies, frees, and saves. We shall make this clearer in a moment. In the meantime, it should be pointed out that the entire Scripture of God is divided into two parts: commands and promises. Commands, to be sure, teach what is good, but what is taught is not thereby done. For the commands show what we ought to do but do not give the power to do it. They were instead established for this: so that they may reveal individuals to themselves. Through the commands they know their inability to do good, and they despair of their own powers. This explains why commands are called and indeed are the *old* testament.[69]

**68.** Here and in the appendix, Luther uses the word *ceremonies* for all types of religious rules and regulations, not just for liturgical rites.

**69.** Emphasis added. It would appear that in this context Luther, rather than referring strictly to the books of the Old and New Testaments, equates "old testament" with any part of the Bible that commands something and "new testament" for language that contains God's promises. For Luther's later reflections on the relation between the Old and New Testaments, see *How Christians Should Regard Moses* (1525) in LW 35:155-74.

c    Luther paraphrases v. 23 and then v. 22 of the Vulgate, adding the term "word." The Vulgate reads: "An abbreviated completion will overflow with righteousness. For the Lord God will make a completion and an abbreviation of troubles in the midst of all the earth." The NRSV states: "Destruction is decreed, overflowing with righteousness. For the Lord God of hosts will make a full end, as decreed, in all the earth." Here Luther treats this text, which refers to a remnant of believing Israel that will survive Assyria's destruction, allegorically.

d    Luther introduced this theme earlier. See p. 492.

### All Commands Are Equally Impossible for Us [70]

For example, "you shall not covet"[71,e] is a command that convicts us all of being sinners, because no one can avoid coveting, no matter how hard we might struggle against it. Thus, in order to keep this commandment and not covet, individuals are forced to despair of themselves and to seek help elsewhere from someone else. As it says in Hos. [13:9]: "Destruction is your own, O Israel. Your help is only in me."[f] However, what occurs with this single commandment occurs in the same way with them all. For all of them are equally impossible for us.

### The Law Must Be Satisfied

Now, when through the commands individuals have been made aware of their powerlessness and now become anxious about how to satisfy the law (since the law must be satisfied so that "not one letter, not one stroke of a letter, will pass away"[g]—otherwise every person would be condemned without hope), they are then humbled and reduced to nothing in their own eyes. They find nothing in themselves by which to be justified and saved. At this point, the second part of Scripture (God's promises, which announce God's glory) arrives and says: "If you want to fulfill the law, 'You shall not covet,' as the law demands, then look here! Believe in Christ, in whom grace, righteousness, peace, freedom, and all things are promised to you. If you believe, you will have these things; if you do not believe, you will lack them."

### We Fulfill Everything through Faith

For what is impossible for you to fulfill using all the works of the law, which though great in number are useless, you will fulfill easily and quickly through faith. Because God the Father has made all things depend on faith, whoever has

**70.** Luther is contradicting Jerome (c. 347–420), who in debates with Augustine (354–430) insisted that commands could be fulfilled, though not without God's grace.

**71.** See the discussion of this commandment in Rom. 7:7-13. See Luther's similar explanation of the Romans passage in his 1522 preface to the book for his German translation of the New Testament (LW 35:376-77).

e   Exod. 20:17.

f   Luther cites the Vulgate, which mirrors the Greek and Syriac. Following the Hebrew, the NRSV has: "I will destroy you, O Israel; who can help you?"

g   Matt. 5:18.

faith has everything and whoever lacks faith has nothing. "For God has imprisoned all in unbelief, so that he may be merciful to all" (Rom. 11[:32]).[h] Thus, God's promises give what the law demands, so that everything may belong to God alone, both the commands and their fulfillment.

### God Alone Commands and Fulfills[72]

God alone commands, and God alone fulfills. Therefore the promises of God pertain to and, indeed, are the *new* testament.[i]

### The First Power of Faith

Now since these promises of God are holy, true, righteous, peaceful, and filled with total goodness, what happens is this: The soul that adheres to them with a firm faith is not simply united with them but fully swallowed up by them, so that it not only shares in them but also is saturated and intoxicated by their every power. For if Christ's touch healed, how much more will this tender touch in the spirit—or, better, this ingestion by the word—communicate to the soul all things that belong to the word. Therefore, by this means, through faith alone without works, the word of God justifies the soul and makes it holy, true, peaceful, and free, filled with every blessing and truly made a child of God, just as John 1[:12] says: "To all who . . . believe in his name, he gave power to become the children of God."

From these arguments it is easy to understand the source of faith's singular ability and why any good work—or all of them put together—cannot equal it at all. Why? Because no good work can cling to the word of God or even exist in the soul. Instead, faith alone and the word rule in it. For the word is of such a nature that the soul is formed by it. Just as heated iron glows like fire because of its union with fire, so it is clear that a Christian needs faith for everything and

72. This sentiment echoes Augustine's famous prayer in the *Confessions* X:29: "Give what you command, and command what you will."

---

*h*    Luther cites the Vulgate. NRSV has "in disobedience."
*i*    Emphasis added. See above, p. 494, n. 69.

will have no need of works to be justified. Now if works are unnecessary, then so is the law. If the law is unnecessary, then certainly such a person is free from the law. Moreover, it is true that "the law is not laid down for the righteous."[j] So, this is the Christian freedom referred to above, namely, our faith, which does not cause us to be lazy and lead evil lives but instead makes the law and works unnecessary for the righteousness and salvation of the Christian.[73]

**73.** Here Luther summarizes the first major theme of this tract and hints at the second (p. 510).

## The Second Power of Faith

Let this suffice for the first power of faith. Let us now look at the second. Faith functions also in the following way. It honors the one in whom it trusts[k] with the most reverent and highest regard possible for this reason: Faith holds the one in whom it trusts to be truthful and deserving.

### The Highest Honor

For no honor is equal to attributing truthfulness and righteousness to someone, which is how we honor the one in whom we trust. Could we ascribe to anyone anything greater than truthfulness, righteousness, and absolutely perfect goodness?

### The Highest Contempt

Conversely, the greatest contempt is to suspect or to accuse someone publicly of being, in our opinion, a liar and wicked, which we do when we do not trust a person. So when the soul firmly believes the God who promises, it regards God as true and righteous. Nothing can show God greater respect!

---

*j*   1 Tim. 1:9, cited according to the Vulgate, which mirrors a literal translation of the Greek. NRSV has "for the innocent."

*k*   The phrase *credere in* (literally, "to believe in") in this paragraph is best rendered "to trust." See Luther's comments on the equivalent German phrase (*glauben an*) in his *A Short Form of the Ten Commandments, Creed and Lord's Prayer* (1520), later printed in his *Personal Prayer Book* (1522) in LW 43:24: "The second kind of faith means believing in God—not just that I believe that what is said about God is true, but that I put my trust in him."

This is the highest worship of God: To bestow on God truthfulness and righteousness and whatever else ought to be ascribed to the One in whom a person trusts. Here the soul submits itself to what God wishes; here it hallows God's name and allows itself to be treated according to God's good pleasure. This is because, clinging to God's promises, the soul does not doubt that God is true, righteous, and wise—the One who will do, arrange, and care for everything in the best possible way.

### Perfect Obedience

Is not such a soul completely obedient to God in all things by this very faith? What commandment remains that such obedience has not completely fulfilled? What fulfillment is fuller than obedience in every situation?[l] However, not works but faith alone offers this obedience.

### Rebellion

Conversely, what greater rebellion against God, godlessness, and contempt of God is there than not to believe the One who promises? What is this but either to make God out a liar or to doubt that God is truthful? Or, to put it another way, is this not to ascribe truthfulness to oneself and falsehood and vanity to God? In so doing, is one not denying God and setting oneself up as an idol in one's very heart? Of what good are works done in this state of godlessness, even if they were angelic and apostolic works? Therefore, God rightly "imprisons everything under unbelief," not under anger or lust,[m] so that people do not imagine that by chaste and gentle works of the law[74] they fulfill the law (granted that such things are civic and human virtues). Such people assume they will be saved, even though they are caught in

74. The opposite of anger and lust. See Luther's commentary on Gal. 5:22 in his *Commentary on Galatians* (1519) in LW 27:377-78, where he condemns works of the law.

l  Luther plays on the words for "fulfill," "fulfillment," and "fuller" (*impleverit, plenitudo, plenior*).

m  Referring to Rom. 11:32, cited above.

the sin of unbelief and must thus either seek mercy or be justly condemned.

### God Honors Those Who Believe in Him

But when God sees that we ascribe truthfulness to him and by our heart's faith honor him as is his due, then in return God honors us, ascribing to us truthfulness and righteousness on account of this faith. For faith results in truthfulness and righteousness, giving to God his own.[75] Thus, in return God gives glory to our righteousness. For it is true and righteous that God is true and righteous, and to ascribe this to God and to confess it means being true and righteous.[n] As 1 Sam. 2[:30] states: "For the ones who honor me I will honor, and those who despise me shall be treated with contempt." As Paul says in Rom. 4[:3] that Abraham's faith "was reckoned to him as righteousness," because through it he fully gave God the glory. For the same reason, if we believe it will be reckoned to us as righteousness.

## The Third Benefit of Faith:
## Union with the Bridegroom[76,o]

The third incomparable benefit[77] of faith is this: that it unites the soul with Christ, like a bride with a bridegroom. By this "mystery" (as Paul teaches),[p] Christ and the soul are made one flesh. For if they are one flesh and if a true marriage—indeed by far the most perfect marriage of all—is culminated between them (since human marriages are but

---

n   Given the standard definition of justice, *iustus* could be translated here "just" rather than "righteous."

o   Combining consecutive marginal notes from the 2d ed.

p   Luther uses here the term *sacramentum*, found in the Vulgate's translation of Eph. 5:32, applying what was said about the church to the soul. This translation of the Greek *mysterion* led eventually to the designation of certain rites in the church as sacraments (literally, in Latin, "oaths" or "vows" but also "mysteries"). First, in the 1522 German translation of the New Testament, Luther renders the phrase "secret" (*Geheimnis*), in line with the Greek, while adding a marginal comment noting the Latin and Greek words.

**75.** Throughout this discussion of faith's second power, Luther uses a standard definition of *iustitia* (righteousness or justice), proposed by Aristotle (384–322 BCE) and employed by Cicero and the Latin legal tradition, as "giving to each his [or her] own." Here, however, by attributing to God truth and righteousness (literally, "God's own"), the soul then receives them back from God as a divine gift. See also his preface to Romans in his translation of the New Testament (1522), in LW 35:371.

**76.** Luther borrows the marital image not only from Ephesians 5 and traditional Christian interpretations of the Song of Songs but more directly from Augustine's *Expositions on the Book of Psalms*, which Luther used in his lectures on the Psalms from 1513 to 1515. See, e.g., Augustine's comments on Ps. 38:3 (Vulgate: 37), par. 5 (English translation in NPNF ser. 1, 14 vols., 8:104), and Luther's glosses on the same psalm (WA 55/1:329). The union of the soul and Christ is also found in many medieval thinkers, including Bernard of Clairvaux and Johannes Tauler (c. 1300–1361).

**77.** In keeping with medieval usage, Luther can still use the word *grace* (*gratia*; here translated as "benefit") as a "bestowed power" and thus a synonym of the word *virtus*, the term for the first two "powers" of faith. By 1521 he would accept Erasmus's argument that in the Greek New Testament the word *charis* (traditionally translated *gratia*) means God's favor (*favor Dei*) or, as the Wittenberg reformers often rendered it, God's mercy (*misericordia Dei*). For

Luther's early, still critical comments on Erasmus's proposal, see the commentary on Galatians (1519) in LW 27:252; and for his acceptance of it two years later, see the tract *Against Latomus* (1521) in LW 32:226–28.

**78.** Luther uses this traditional language about the marriage of Christ and the soul to illustrate his understanding of justification by faith. Roman marriage law distinguished between property (what one owned) and possession (what one had full use of) and held that in marriage the property of the one spouse became the possession of the other and vice versa. Similarly, Luther argues here and in the ensuing paragraphs that what is Christ's own (grace, life, and salvation) becomes the soul's and what is the soul's own (sin, death, and damnation) becomes Christ's, all by the marriage of faith. Luther first published his thoughts on this "joyous exchange" (the phrase used in the German version of *The Freedom of a Christian*) in *Two Kinds of Righteousness* (1519) in LW 31:297–99, a forerunner to this tract, although he employed it earlier in the lecture hall, pulpit, and correspondence. For one example, see the letter to Georg Spenlein (1486–1563) from 8 April 1516 (LW 48:12–13).

**79.** Luther's description of the extended metaphor of Christ's battle against sin for his bride is reminiscent of chivalry.

weak shadows of this one), then it follows that they come to hold all things, good and bad, in common. Accordingly, the faithful soul can both assume as its own whatever Christ has and glory in it, and whatever is the soul's Christ claims for himself as his own.[78]

### Consider These Invaluable Things!

Let us examine these things in detail to see how invaluable they are. Christ is full of grace, life, and salvation; the soul is full of sins, death, and damnation. Now let faith intervene and it will turn out that sins, death, and hell are Christ's, but grace, life, and salvation are the soul's. For if he is the groom, then he should simultaneously both accept the things belonging to the bride and impart to the bride those things that are his. For the one who gives his body and his very self to her, how does he not give his all? And the one who receives the body of the bride, how does he not take all that is hers?[q]

### Love's Duel in Christ

This is truly the most delightful drama,[79,r] involving not only communion but also a saving war, victory, salvation, and redemption. For Christ is God and a human being in one and the same person, who does not and cannot sin, die, or be damned; and his righteousness, life, and salvation are unconquerable, eternal, and all-powerful. When, I say, such a person shares in common and, indeed, takes as his own the sins, death, and hell of the bride on account of the wedding ring of faith, and when he regards them as if they were his own and as if he himself had sinned—suffering, dying, and descending into hell—then, as he conquers them all and as sin, death, and hell cannot devour him, they are devoured by

q    Here, among other things, Luther echoes the language of 1 Cor. 7:4.
r    Latin: *spectaculum*, literally, "a piece of theater."

him in an astounding duel.[80] For his righteousness is superior to all sins, his life more powerful than death, and his salvation more invincible than hell.

### The Wedding Ring of Faith for the Bride of Christ

So it happens that the faithful soul, through the wedding ring of its faith in Christ her bridegroom, is free from all sins, secure against death, protected from hell, and given the eternal righteousness, life, and salvation of her bridegroom, Christ. Thus, "he takes to himself a glorious bride without spot or wrinkle . . . making her clean by washing . . . in the word of life,"[s] that is, through faith in the word, life, righteousness, and salvation [of Christ]. As Hos. 2[:19] says, [the Lord] becomes engaged to her "in faith, in mercy and compassion, in righteousness, and judgment."[t]

### The Majesty of the Wedding Garments

Who can even begin to appreciate this royal marriage? What can comprehend the riches of this glorious grace? Here, this rich, upstanding bridegroom, Christ, marries this poor, disloyal little prostitute, redeems her from all her evil and adorns her with all his goodness. For now it is impossible for her sins to destroy her, because they have been laid upon Christ and devoured by him. In Christ, her bridegroom, she has her righteousness, which she can enjoy as her very own property. And with confidence she can set this righteousness over against all of her sins and in opposition to death and hell and can say, "Sure, I have sinned, but my Christ, in whom I trust, has not sinned. All that is his is mine and all that is mine is his." As it says in the Song of Sol. [2:16]: "My beloved is mine, and I am his." This is what Paul says in

**80.** This image of Christ as victor, popular among many Greek fathers and Augustine, was overshadowed in medieval theology by other explanations. Luther, however, uses this notion throughout his career. For just two examples of many, see his hymn "A Mighty Fortress" or his commentary on Gal. 3:13 (1535) in LW 26:276–91.

---

s    A fairly close rendering of Eph. 5:27a and 26b, leaving out the words "church" and "water."

t    This citation matches the Vulgate: "And I will take you as my wife in righteousness and judgment and in mercy and in compassion, and I will take you as my wife in faith."

1 Cor. 15[:57]: "Thanks be to God, who gives us the victory through our Lord Jesus Christ." But this "victory" is over sin and death, as he notes in the previous verse [v. 56]: "The sting of death is sin, and the power of sin is the law."

### Why Ascribe These Things Only to Faith? [u]

From the preceding, you may once again understand why the fulfillment of the law and justification without any works by faith alone may only be ascribed to faith. You observe that the first commandment, "You shall worship one God," is fulfilled by faith alone.[81]

#### True Worship of God

For even if you were nothing but good works from the soles of your feet to the top of your head, you would still not be righteous, worship God, or fulfill the first commandment, since God cannot be worshiped unless the glory of truth and of complete goodness is ascribed to him, as truly must be due him.

#### Faith Does Works [v]

But works cannot do this—only faith of the heart can. For not by working but by believing do we glorify God and confess that God is truthful. On this basis, faith alone is the righteousness of a Christian and the fulfilling of all the commandments, because the one who fulfills the first commandment easily fulfills all the works of the others. Now works, being inanimate, cannot glorify God, although they can be done to God's glory if faith is present.[82] At this juncture, however, we are not asking about the kinds of works that are to be done but about the person who does them, who glorifies God and who produces works. This faith of the

**81.** This reflects Luther's interpretation of the first commandment, already expressed earlier in 1520 in his *Treatise on Good Works* (see pp. 267–86) and later in his catechisms of 1529.

**82.** Luther here distinguishes works, the fruits of faith, which he labels inanimate, from faith itself, which is alive in the heart of the believer. Works for him are an effect of faith; faith is the cause.

---

u    This section summarizes Luther's argument regarding the three powers of faith.

v    This refers to the second power of faith. See above, p. 497.

heart is the source and substance of all of our righteousness. Thus, it is a blind and dangerous instruction that teaches works must fulfill the commandments, because the commandments must be fulfilled before all works and thus works follow this fulfillment, as we will hear.[w]

### The Prerogatives of the Firstborn[83]

In order to examine more closely this grace that our inner person possesses in Christ, it must be realized that God in the Old Testament consecrated to himself all firstborn males. And this birthright was highly prized, giving power over all others with a double honor: priesthood and kingship.[84] The firstborn brother was a priest and ruler over all others. This figure foreshadowed Christ who, as the true and only firstborn of God the Father and of the Virgin Mary, was true king and priest but not according to the flesh and this world.

#### What Christ's Kingdom and Priesthood Consist In[x]

For his "kingdom is not from this world."[y] He rules over and consecrates heavenly and spiritual things, such as righteousness, truth, wisdom, peace, and salvation. Not that everything on earth and in hell is not subjected to him (otherwise, how could he protect and save us from them?), but his kingdom does not consist in nor is it derived from such things. Similarly, his priesthood does not consist in the external pomp of robes and gestures, as did that human priesthood of Aaron then and as our ecclesiastical priesthood does today. But his consists in spiritual things, through which, in an invisible, heavenly office, he intercedes for us before God, offers himself there, and does all the things that a priest ought to do.

**83.** Here Luther introduces a new argument. For the law of the primogeniture of priests, see Exod. 13:2. For the primogeniture of kings, see, e.g., the struggle of succession at the time of David's death in 1 Kings 1–2 (esp. 2:22). Luther, following the longstanding practice of the church, views these historical facts in the Old Testament as types or figures, pointing to Christ.

**84.** Throughout, the word *sacerdos* is translated "priest," a term used in the Old Testament for the official priests and in the New only for Christ or for all believers in him. The word *priest* in English (as in many other European languages) is derived from the Greek word *presbyteros* ("elder").

---

w   See the second major theme on p. 510 below.

x   Combining two marginal glosses (2d ed.).

y   John 18:36.

## The Priestly Office

This is how Paul describes him in Hebrews [7], using the figure of Melchizedek.[z] Not only does he pray and intercede for us, but he also teaches us inwardly in the spirit by the living instruction of his Spirit. These two things are properly speaking the offices of a priest that are prefigured by the visible prayers and sermons of human priests.

### How Faithful Christians Ought to Be Understood as Priests and Kings[a]

Now, just as Christ by his birthright possessed these two ranks, so he imparts them to and shares them with every believer legally in accord with the marriage described above, where whatever are the bridegroom's belong to the bride. Hence, all of us who trust in Christ are all priests and kings in Christ, as 1 Pet. 2[:9] states: "You are a chosen race, an acquired people, a royal priesthood and a priestly kingdom, so that you may recount the powers of the one who called you from darkness into his marvelous light."[b] The nature of these two ranks is as follows.

### The Spiritual Kingdom[c]

First, what pertains to kingship is this: through faith every Christian is exalted over all things and, by virtue of spiritual power, is absolutely lord of all things. Consequently, nothing at all can ever harm such a one to whom, indeed, all things are subject and forced to serve for salvation. Paul states this in Rom. 8[:28]: "We know that all things work together for

---

z  Based upon Genesis 14 and Ps. 110:4. The authorship of Hebrews was contested in the sixteenth century, so that on other occasions Luther admitted that Paul did not write this letter.

a  Combining two marginal glosses (2d ed.).

b  Here Luther follows the Vulgate, replacing "holy nation" with "priestly nation" and "announce" with "recount." Luther also uses this text in his *Address to the Christian Nobility* (p. 382).

c  Mg. (2d ed.), moved slightly to correspond to the text.

good for the elect."[d] He says the same thing in 1 Cor. 3[:21b-23]: "All things are yours, whether . . . life or death or the present or the future . . . and you belong to Christ."

## Note!

Now, this does not establish that Christians possess and exercise some sort of secular[e] power over everything—ecclesiastical leaders far and wide are possessed by such madness—for this is something that belongs to kings, princes, and human beings on earth.[f] We see from our daily experience in life that we are subjected to all kinds of things, suffer many things, and even die. Indeed, the more Christian a person is, the more he or she is subject to evils, suffering, or death, as we see in Christ, the firstborn prince himself, and in all his holy brothers [and sisters].

This power, which "rules in the midst of enemies"[g] and is powerful "in the midst of oppression,"[h] is spiritual. This is nothing other than "power made perfect in weakness" so that in "all things . . . I may gain" salvation.[i] In this way, the cross and death are forced to serve me and to work together for salvation. This is a lofty, splendid high rank and a true, omnipotent power and a spiritual sovereignty, in which there is nothing so good or nothing so evil that cannot "work together for good,"[j] if only I believe. Still, because faith alone suffices for salvation, I do not need anything else except for faith exercising its power and sovereignty of freedom in these things. Look here! This is the immeasurable power and freedom of Christians.

d  NRSV: "for those who love God." Reference to the elect comes in the following verse.
e  The word *corporali*, translated "secular," is literally, "bodily" or "physical."
f  Luther expanded this distinction in 1523 in *On Secular Authority* (LW 45:75–129).
g  Ps. 110:2.
h  An allusion to 2 Cor. 4:8 as rendered in Erasmus's Latin translation of the Greek.
i  Allusions to 2 Cor. 12:9 and Phil. 3:9.
j  Rom. 8:28.

### *We Are Priests Forever* [k]

Not only are we the freest kings of all, but we are also priests forever. This is more excellent by far than kingship, because through the priesthood we are worthy to appear before God, to pray for others, and to teach one another the things that are of God. For these are the priestly duties that absolutely cannot be bestowed on anyone who does not believe. Christ obtained this priesthood for us, if we trust in him, so that as we are confreres, coheirs, corulers, so we are co-priests with him, daring to come with confidence into God's presence in the spirit of faith and cry, "Abba, Father," [l] to pray for another and to do all the things that we see are done and prefigured by the visible and corporeal office of priests.

### *Only Evil Comes to Nonbelievers*

But nothing serves persons who do not believe, nor does anything "work together for good." [m] Instead, such individuals are slaves of all things and give themselves over to evil, because they use everything wickedly for their own advantage and not to the glory of God. Thus, they are not priests but profane people. Their prayers become sin, nor do they appear in God's presence, because God does not listen to sinners. Who, therefore, can comprehend the height of this Christian rank, which through its regal power is lord of all things—death, life, sin, and the like—but through its priestly glory can do all things before God, because God does what the priest asks and desires? As it is written: "He fulfills the desire of all who fear him; he also hears their cry, and saves them." [n] A person certainly arrives at this glory not by works but by faith alone.

---

k    Referring back to Ps. 110:4.

l    Rom. 8:15.

m    Rom. 8:28. Luther uses the singular ("a" person) throughout this paragraph.

n    Ps. 145:19.

## The Freedom of Christians[85]

From the foregoing, anyone can clearly see how the Christian is free from all things and is over all things, so that such a person requires no works at all to be righteous or saved. Instead, faith alone bestows all these things in abundance. Now, if someone were so foolish as to presume to be made righteous, free, saved, and Christian through any good work, then such one would immediately lose faith along with all other good things. This foolishness is beautifully illustrated in that fable where a dog runs along a stream holding a piece of real meat in his mouth. When, deceived by the reflection of the meat in the water, the dog tries to get it by opening its mouth and loses both the meat and the reflection.[86]

## [A Digression on the Meaning of Priesthood][87]

At this point, you may ask, "If all people in the church are priests, by what name do we distinguish those we now call priests from the laity?" I respond that an injustice has been done to these words—"priest," "cleric," "a spiritual one," and "a churchman"—when they are transferred from all other Christians to those few who now are called by this faulty usage "churchmen."[88] For Holy Scripture does not distinguish at all among them, except that it calls "ministers," "servants" and "stewards" those who now are proudly labeled popes, bishops, and lords but who should be serving others with the ministry of the word in order to teach the faith of Christ and the freedom of the faithful. For, although it is true that we are all equally priests, nevertheless we cannot all serve and teach nor, even if we can, ought we all to do so publicly. As Paul states in 1 Cor. 4[:1]: "Let a person regard us as servants of Christ and dispensers of God's mysteries."[o]

85. This begins the conclusion to the first major theme, which Luther picks up again after the digression on priesthood and then applies it to preaching.

86. Luther filled his writings with allusions to classical sources, including *Aesop's Fables*, as here. His 1530 translation of these fables was published in 1557 (WA 50:432-60).

87. This subtitle was not in any sixteenth-century text. These two paragraphs form a digression from Luther's main argument, in order to discuss the proper meaning of "priest" (*sacerdos*). See also his discussion of what later became known as the "priesthood of all believers" in the *Address to the Christian Nobility* (pp. 382-84).

88. Although his main interest is in the use of the word *priest* (*sacerdos*), Luther employs other common terms for the ordained here: *cleros* ("cleric," a loan word into ecclesiastical Latin from the Greek, designating the clergy), *spiritualis* (a spiritual person [both priests and monks], as opposed to the laity, who live in the world) and *ecclesiasticus* ("ecclesiast," a church official [especially a teacher or preacher], but literally, "one who belongs to the church").

---

*o*   Reading with the Vulgate.

*What the Ministry of Churchmen Has Become*

Against this, such "dispensing" has now turned into such a display of power and a terrible tyranny that no national or worldly political power can be compared to it. It is as if the laity were something other than Christians. As a result of this perversity, the knowledge of Christian grace, faith, freedom, and Christ has perished entirely, only to be replaced by an intolerable captivity to human works and laws. As the Lamentations of Jeremiah puts it, we have become slaves of the vilest possible people on earth, who abuse our misery in all baseness and degradation of their desire.*p*

### How Christ Must Be Preached

To return to my main topic, I believe that it has become clear that it is not sufficient or even Christian if, as those who are the very best preachers today do, we only preach Christ's works, life, and words just as a kind of story or as historical exploits (which would be enough to know for an example of how to conduct our lives). Much worse is when there is complete silence about Christ and human laws, and the decrees of the fathers[89] are taught instead of Christ. Moreover, some even preach Christ and recite stories about him for this purpose: to play on human emotions either to arouse sympathy for him or to incite anger against the Jews.[90] This kind of thing is simply childish and womanish nonsense.[91] Preaching, however, ought to serve this goal: that faith in Christ is promoted. Then he is not simply "Christ" but "Christ for you and me," and what we say about him and call him affect us.[92] This faith is born and preserved by preaching why Christ came, what he brought and gave, and what are the needs and the fruit that his reception entail. This kind of preaching occurs where Christian freedom, which we gain from him and which makes us Christians all kings and priests, is rightly taught. In him we are lords of all, and we trust that whatever we might do is pleasing and acceptable in God's sight, as we said above.

89. Luther was probably thinking of canon law, the church rules from ancient and medieval teachers, popes, and councils that regulated the practice of penance, marriage, and all other aspects of church life.

90. For Luther's earlier criticism of this kind of preaching during Holy Week, see *A Meditation on Christ's Passion* (p. 169).

91. Luther assumes, as did most men of his time (following Aristotle among others), that the emotions of children and women are especially easily manipulated by such preaching.

92. Luther reflects this conviction in comments about Christ in his catechisms, where he speaks of Christ as "my Lord, who redeemed me."

p   Perhaps an allusion to Lamentations 1 or to the entire book.

### The Fruit of the Best Preaching[q]

What person's heart upon hearing these things would not rejoice from its very core and upon accepting such consolation would not melt[r] in love with Christ—something completely unattainable with laws and works? Who could possibly harm or frighten such a heart? If awareness of sin or dread of death overwhelms it, it is ready to hope in the Lord. It neither fears hearing about these evils nor is moved by them, until finally it despises its enemies.[s] For it believes that Christ's righteousness is its own and that its sin is now not its own but Christ's. More than that, the presence[t] of Christ's righteousness swallows up every sin. As noted above, this is a necessary consequence of faith in Christ. So the heart learns with the Apostle to scoff at death and sin and to say: "Where, O death, is your victory? Where, O death, is your sting? The sting of death is sin, and the power of sin is the law. But thanks be to God, who gives us the victory through our Lord Jesus Christ."[u] For death is swallowed up in victory—not only Christ's but ours—because through faith it becomes our victory and is in us and we are conquerors.

In a scene from the 1530 edition of the *Large Catechism* printed in Wittenberg, a preacher addresses a congregation from the pulpit, illustrating the petition in the Lord's Prayer, "Hallowed be your name."

q   Luther moves from what preaching is to its effects.
r   Literally, "become sweet."
s   Perhaps an allusion to Ps. 110:1.
t   Literally, "face."
u   1 Cor. 15:55-57.

Enough now has been said about the inner person, its freedom and its origin in the righteousness of faith. This inner person requires neither laws nor good works, which are harmful to it whenever someone presumes to be justified through them.

## [The Outer Person][93, v]

**93.** This begins the second main section of the tract on the second of the two themes introduced above (p. 489).

Let us now turn to the second part, which concerns the outer person. Here we will respond to all those people who are offended by the word of faith and what has been said about it. They say, "If faith does all things and alone suffices for righteousness, why then are good works commanded? We will therefore be content with faith, take our ease and do no works." I respond, "Not so, you wicked people, not so!"[94] To be sure, this would be true if we were completely and perfectly inner, spiritual persons, which will not happen until the resurrection of the dead on the last day. As long as we live in the flesh, we are only beginning and advancing toward what will be perfected in the future life. The Apostle in Romans 8[:23] calls this the "first fruits of the Spirit," because in this life we will have received only a tenth but in the future life the fullness of the Spirit. So, this part of the essay pertains to what was said at the beginning: The Christian is a slave of all and subject to all.[w] Insofar as a Christian is free, he or she does nothing; insofar as the Christian is a slave, he or she does all things. Now we shall see how this can happen.

**94.** Luther is attacking moralistic opponents for pretending to make this argument as a way of destroying Christian freedom.

To be sure, as I have said, the inner person is in the spirit fully and completely justified through faith. Such a one has what he or she ought to have, except of course that this very faith and its riches ought to increase day by day toward the future life. For now, however, this person remains in this

---

v   This subtitle was not in any sixteenth-century text. Instead, the marginal gloss in the second edition reads: "A question from those who do not understand Luther—or rather—what faith is."

w   See above, p. 488.

mortal life on earth. In this life a person's own body must be ruled and be in relation with other human beings.

## Where Works Begin [95]

Now here is where works begin. Here is not the time for leisure; here care must be taken to train the body by means of fasting, vigils, and other labors and to subdue it by the spirit.[96] In this way it may obey and be conformed to the inner person and faith, so that it may not rebel against or impede the inner person (as is its nature when not held in check).

### The Single Concern of the Inner Person

For the inner person—conformed to God and created in the image of God through faith—is joyful and glad on account of Christ, in whom all good things have been conferred upon such a one. Because of this, that person has only one concern: to serve God joyfully, with boundless love and with no thought of earning anything. While acting this way, immediately the inner creature offends a contrary will in its own flesh, one that serves the world and tries seeking after what belongs to it. Because the spirit of faith cannot tolerate this at all, it attempts with joyful zeal to suppress and coerce the flesh. As Paul says in Rom. 7[:22-23]: "I delight in the law of God according to my inner person,[x] but I see in my members another law fighting against the law of my mind and making me captive to the law of sin." In another place,[y] he writes, "I punish my body and enslave it, so that after proclaiming to others I myself should not be disqualified." And in Gal. 5[:24] he states, "And those who belong to Christ Jesus have crucified the flesh with its passions and desires."[97]

95. Here begins the first part of the second major theme on discipline of the flesh and works in general. For the second part (on love of neighbor), see below, p. 519.

96. Luther alludes to common practices of the day designed to restrain the flesh.

97. Throughout this section, Luther uses the technical term *concupiscentia*, translated here "desire." Concupiscence was said by medieval theologians to be the "matter" of sin that remained after baptism. Without the "form" of the willing conscience willing a sinful act, it was not viewed as sin. Luther and Reformation theologians rejected the imposition of medieval Aristotelian categories and insisted that such desires were themselves already sin. Thus, already in the lectures on Romans (1515–1516), in LW 25:336, and throughout his career (e.g., in the commentary on Galatians [1535] in LW 26:232), Luther declared that the justified person was *simul iustus et peccator* (at the same time justified and sinner).

---

x    Reading with the Vulgate.

y    1 Cor. 9:27.

*Under What Supposition Are Works to Be Done?*

These works, however, ought not to be done under the supposition that through them a person is justified before God. For faith, which alone is righteousness before God, does not endure this false opinion but supposes [that works be done] only so that "the body may be enslaved" and may be purified from its evil "passions and desires" so that the eye may not turn again to these expunged desires.[z] Because the soul has been cleansed through faith and made to love God, at the same time it wants all things (in particular the body) to be cleansed, so that all things may love and praise God with it. As a result, the human creature cannot be idle because of the demands of its body, and, because of the body, it attempts to do many good things to bring it under control. Nevertheless, these works are not what justify someone before God. Instead, the person does them in compliance to God out of spontaneous love, considering nothing else than the divine favor to which the person wishes to comply most dutifully in all things.

## How to Discipline the Body

For this reason, all individuals[a] can easily figure out for themselves the "measure or discretion" (as people call it)[98,b] to which they ought to discipline their bodies. For they may only fast, perform vigils, and labor to the extent that they see it to be necessary for suppressing the body's wantonness and desire. Those who presume to be justified by works, however, have no regard for extinguishing[c] desires but only for the works themselves. They suppose that if they do so many great works, then they will fare well and be made righteous— sometimes even injuring their minds and destroying or at least rendering useless what makes them human. Wanting

**98.** Here Luther uses traditional language in relation to the freedom of faith, allowing the individual believer, not the confessor, to determine how much to discipline the body. See already his *Treatise on Good Works*, above, p. 324.

---

z    Cf. 1 Cor. 9:27; Gal. 5:24; and 1 John 2:16.

a    In the singular in the original.

b    Latin: *mensura aut discretio*. This phrase is found in medieval books on virtues and vices and in medieval penitential manuals.

c    Latin: *mortificatio*.

to be justified and saved through works without faith is simply monstrous foolishness and ignorance of the Christian life and faith!

### An Excellent Analogy

So that we may make it easier to understand what we have said, let us illustrate these things with some analogies. The works of Christian individuals,*d* who are justified and saved through their faith by the pure and gracious mercy of God, ought not be considered from any other perspective than would be the works of Adam and Eve and their children had they not sinned. This is talked about in Gen. 2[:15]: God "placed the man," whom he had formed, "in paradise . . . so that he might work and take care of it."*e* Now, God created Adam to be righteous, upright, and without sin, so that through his work and care he had no need to be justified or made upright. Rather, so that he would not become idle, the Lord gave him a job, namely, that he care for and watch over paradise. These were truly the freest works, done neither "to make [a person] acceptable to anyone"[99] (except to divine favor) nor to obtain righteousness, which Adam already had fully and which would have been inborn in all of us.

### Faith Puts a Person Back in Paradise

It is the same way with works of believing individuals,*f* who through their faith are once again put back in paradise and recreated from scratch. They would not do works to become or to be righteous but in order not to be idle and "to work and watch over" their bodies. For them these works arise

In this engraving from a 1545 Leipzig publication of Luther's *Small Catechism*, God is shown marrying Adam and Eve.

**99.** Medieval theologians defined justifying grace as *gratia gratum faciens*, the grace that makes acceptable, namely, by infusing a disposition (*habitus*) of love (*charitas*) into the soul and thus moving the soul from a state of mortal sin into a state of grace. Such a person then did good works acceptable to God.

---

*d*  Singular in the original text.

*e*  Cited according to the Vulgate.

*f*  In the singular throughout this paragraph in the original.

from the same freedom [as Adam's], done only in consideration of divine favor—except that we are not yet fully recreated with perfect faith and love, which ought to increase not through works but through themselves.

### Another Comparison

Here is another analogy. When a consecrated bishop dedicates a church building, confirms children, or performs some other duty pertaining to his office, he is not consecrated into office by performing these very works. Far from it! Unless he had already been consecrated a bishop beforehand, all of these works would be worthless; they would instead be foolish, childish, and silly. So also individual Christians,[g] who are consecrated by their faith, do good works, but through them they are not made holy[h] or Christian. For this arises from faith alone; indeed, unless they believed and were Christian beforehand, all of their works would be worthless and would be truly ungodly and damnable sins.

### Two Statements Worth Remembering

Therefore, these two sayings are true: "Good works do not make a person good, but a good person does good works," and "Evil[i] works do not make a person evil, but an evil person does evil works." Thus, a person's essence or character must be good before all works, and good works follow and proceed from a good person.[100]

### A Comparison

As Christ also says, "A good tree cannot bear bad fruit, nor can a bad tree bear good fruit."[j] It is obvious that fruit do not bear a tree nor does a tree grow on fruit, but just the reverse: trees bear fruit and fruit grow on trees. Therefore, just as it is necessary that trees exist prior to their fruit and

**100.** This is against the notion in Aristotelian ethics, followed by medieval theologians, that a person becomes good by doing good.

g   In the singular throughout this paragraph in the original text.
h   The same adjective translated "consecrated" above.
i   In these paragraphs the Latin *malum* is translated either "evil" or "bad," depending on the context.
j   Matt. 7:18.

that fruit make trees neither good nor bad, but that, on the contrary, specific kinds of trees make specific kinds of fruit, so it is necessary that first the very character of a person be good or evil before doing any good or evil work and that a person's works do not make one evil or good but rather that a person does evil or good works.

### Another Comparison

Similar things can be seen in construction. A good or bad house does not make a good or bad builder, but a good or bad builder makes a good or bad house. As a general rule, no work makes its kind of artisan, but an artisan makes a particular kind of work. This same reality obtains for the works of human beings. Whatever kind of person one is—either in faith or unbelief—that determines one's work: good if done in faith, evil if done in unbelief. But this may not be reversed: as if whatever the kind of work determines the kind of human being—either in faith or unbelief. For just as works do not make someone a believer,[k] so also they do not make a person righteous. On the contrary, just as faith makes someone a believer and righteous, so also it produces good works.

## Faith Alone Justifies

Since, therefore, works do not justify anyone and a person must be righteous before doing something good, these things are absolutely clear: that faith alone—because of the sheer mercy of God through Christ [given] in his word—properly and completely justifies and saves a person; and that no law is necessary for a Christian's salvation, since through faith one is free from every law and does everything that is done spontaneously, out of sheer freedom. Such a person seeks nothing for a payment or for salvation—already being satisfied and saved by God's grace from one's faith—but seeks only what pleases God.

k    See above, p. 493.

### Unbelievers Do Not Become Evil by Works

In the same way, no good work of an unbeliever contributes toward righteousness or salvation. On the other side, no evil work makes an unbeliever evil or damnable. Instead, unbelief, which makes an evil person and tree, does evil and damnable works. Thus, when someone is good or evil, this arises not from works but from faith or unbelief, as Sir. [10:14] says, "This is the beginning of sin, that a person falls away from God," that is, "does not believe." Paul states in Hebrews 11[:6]: "For whoever would approach God must believe." And Christ says the same thing: "Either make the tree good, and its fruit good; or make the tree bad and its fruit bad,"*l* as if he were saying, "Let whoever wants to have good fruit begin with the tree and plant a good one." Therefore, let whoever wants to do good things begin not with the doing but with the believing. For only faith makes a person good, and only unbelief makes someone evil.

### Works Make a Human Being Good but Only in Human Eyes

To be sure, it is true that in the eyes of other human beings, works make a human being good or evil. But this happens the same way as when it is known or shown that someone is good or evil, as Christ says in Matt. 7[:20], "You will know them by their fruits." But all of this remains external and on the surface, which is just where many who presume to write and teach about "the good works by which we are justified"[101] are led astray.

### The Source of Some Peoples' Error

Meanwhile, they do not even mention faith: going their false ways,*m* always leading astray, "progressing from bad to worse,"*n* "the blind leading the blind,"*o* wearying themselves

101. Luther has in mind especially Gabriel Biel (c. 1420–1495) and Luther's own opponents who followed Biel's argument that a person merited justifying grace. See Heiko A. Oberman, *Harvest of Medieval Theology: Gabriel Biel and Late Medieval Nominalism*, 3d ed. (Durham, NC: Labyrinth, 1983), 141, esp. n.66.

*l*   Matt. 12:23.
*m*  Echoing biblical condemnations, as in 2 Kgs. 8:18.
*n*  Paraphrasing 2 Tim. 3:13.
*o*  Matt. 15:14.

with many works and still never arriving at the true righteousness. Paul speaks about these people in 2 Tim. 3[:5, 7]: "Holding to the outward form of godliness but denying its power . . . who are always being instructed and can never arrive at knowledge of the truth."

Therefore, whoever does not want to fall into the same error with these blind people must look beyond works, laws, and teachings about works. More than that, one must focus on the person completely apart from works and on how such a one is justified. A person is justified and saved not by works or laws but by the Word of God (that is, by the promise of God's grace) and by faith. In this way, what remains firm is the glory of the divine majesty, which saves us who believe not by works of righteousness that we do but in accord with God's mercy through the word of his grace.

*Rules for Understanding the Teachings of Many People Today*
From all that has been said, it is easy to understand on what grounds good works must be rejected or accepted and by what rule everyone's current teachings about good works must be evaluated. For if works are coupled with righteousness and by that perverse Leviathan[102, p] and false persuasion take on such a character that you presume to be justified through them, then they become absolutely compulsory and extinguish freedom along with faith. By this kind of linkage, such works are no longer good but instead truly damnable. For they are not free, and they blaspheme against the grace of God, to whom alone belong justification and salvation through faith. What works are powerless to guarantee, they nevertheless pretend to do by this godless presumption and through this foolishness of ours, and thereby they intrude violently into the function of grace and its glory.

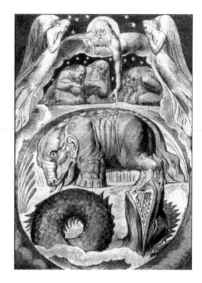

Leviathan and Behemoth.

102. As had medieval interpreters and even the Hebraist Johannes Reuchlin (1455–1522), Luther identifies Leviathan (a monster made up of a perverse mixture of parts) with the combination of sins or improper teachings prompted by the devil. See, e.g., the reference in his earliest lectures on the Psalms (1513–1515) in LW 10:273.

p  See Job 41; Isa. 27:1; Pss. 74:14; 104:26; and Job 3:8.

### The Basis of Luther's Teaching[q]

Therefore, we do not reject good works. On the contrary, we highly cherish and teach them. For we do not condemn them for their own sake but on account of this godless linkage and perverse opinion that try to seek righteousness [through them]. This makes them appear good on the surface when in reality they are not good. By such works people are deceived and, like ravenous wolves in sheep's clothing, they deceive [others].[r]

### The Work of Leviathan

But this Leviathan and perverse opinion about works is impossible to overcome where genuine faith is lacking. These "work-saints" cannot get rid of this [monster] unless faith, its destroyer, comes and rules in the heart. Nature by itself cannot drive it out and, worse yet, cannot even recognize it but rather considers it the ground for the holiest of desires. In this situation, if (as godless teachers have done) custom invokes and strengthens this depravity of nature, it becomes an incurable evil that seduces and destroys countless people irreparably. Thus, while it is fine to preach and write about penitence, confession, and satisfaction,[103] nevertheless, they are without a doubt deceptive and diabolical teachings when placed here [with works] and not derived from faith as taught above.[104] For this is why Christ, like John [the Baptist], did not only say, "Repent,"[s] but added the word of faith, saying: "The kingdom of heaven has come near."[t]

### Faith Ought to Be Awakened in Preaching

For we must preach not only one word of God but both, "bringing forth new and old from the treasure"[u]—both the

---

**103.** Here Luther is referring to the three parts of the sacrament of penance: contrition (sorrow for sin out of love of God), (private) confession, and (works of) satisfaction. For the first part he uses the more general term, *poenitentia*, which can refer either to the entire sacrament or to the sinner's penitence. For the role of penance in the origins of the Reformation, see above, pp. 13–16.

**104.** This reframes Luther's basic argument in the first four of the *95 Theses*. See above, p. 34f.

---

*q*   The second of several marginal glosses from the second edition referring to Luther in the third person. See above, p. 510, note *v*.

*r*   See Matt. 7:15.

*s*   In the Latin Vulgate, the text (*poenitentiam agite*) may be translated either "Do penance" or "Repent."

*t*   Matt. 4:17, also quoted in the *95 Theses*, thesis 1. See above, p. 34.

*u*   Matt. 13:52. In contrast, medieval commentators interpreted "old and new" as the Old and New Testaments. See above, p. 494, n. 94.

voice of the law and the word of grace. The voice of the law ought to be "brought forth" so that people may be terrified and led to a knowledge of their sins and thereby directed toward repentance[v] and a better basis for life. But the word must not stop here. For this would be only "to wound" and not "to bind up"; "to strike down" and not "to heal"; "to kill" and not "to make alive"; "to lead into hell" and not "to lead out"; "to humble" but not "to exalt."[w] Therefore, the word of grace and promised forgiveness ought also to be preached in order to instruct and awaken faith. Without this other word [of grace], law, contrition, penitence, and everything else are done and taught in vain.

### The Origin of Repentance and Faith

To be sure, preachers of repentance and grace are still around, but they do not explain God's law and promise in light of their purpose and spirit, so that people can find out where repentance and grace come from. For repentance arises from God's law, but faith or grace come from the promise of God, as Rom. 10[:17] states: "So faith comes from what is heard, and what is heard comes through the word of Christ." It happens like this: A person, who has been humbled by the threats and fear of the divine law and led to self-knowledge, is consoled and raised up through faith in the divine promise. As Psalm 30[:6] says, "Weeping may linger for the night, but joy comes with the morning."

### Concerning Works for the Neighbor[105]

Up to now we have spoken about works in general and, at the same time, about those specific things that a Christian must do to train his or her own body. Finally, we will discuss those things done for one's neighbor. For a human being does not live in this mortal body solely for himself or herself and work only on it but lives together with all other human

105. What follows constitutes a second major section of this part of the tract. For the first section (on discipline of the flesh), see above, p. 511.

---

v   Latin: *poenitentia*, a word that may be translated as "repentance," "penitence," or the "sacrament of penance."

w   A combination of Deut. 32:39; 1 Sam. 2:6-7; and Hos. 6:1.

beings on earth. Indeed, more to the point, each person lives only for others and not for himself or herself. The purpose of putting the body in subjection is so that it can serve others more genuinely and more freely. As Paul says in Rom. 14[:7-8], "We do not live to ourselves. If we live, we live to the Lord, and if we die, we die to the Lord." Thus, it can never happen that in this life a person is idle and without works toward one's neighbors. For it is necessary to speak, act, and live with other human beings, just as Christ was "made in human likeness and found in human form"[106, x] and "lived with humankind," as Bar. 3[:37] says.[107]

### Serving All People

Nevertheless, no one needs even one of these works to attain righteousness and salvation. For this reason, in all of one's works a person should in this context be shaped by and contemplate this thought alone: to serve and benefit others in everything that may be done, having nothing else in view except the need and advantage of the neighbor. So the Apostle commands that "we work with our hands so that we may give to those in need."[y] Although he could have said, "so that we may support ourselves," he said instead, "give to those in need."

### Why the Body Must Be Taken Care Of

For, under these circumstances, it is also Christian to care for the body. At times when the body is healthy and fit, we can work and save money and thereby can protect and support those who are in need. In this way, the stronger members may serve the weaker[z] and we may be sons [and daughters] of God: one person caring and working for another, "bearing

---

**106.** Luther's references to Phil. 2 throughout the tract suggest its origins as a sermon on the epistle for Palm Sunday. See p. 489, n. 58.

**107.** "Afterward she [Wisdom] appeared on earth and lived with humankind." Already the ancient church associated references to Wisdom (here and in Prov. 8) with Christ. Luther accorded some authority to the Apocrypha, and his complete translation of the Bible into German, first published in 1534, always included the Apocrypha, although his introduction to Baruch in LW 35:349–50 is rather harsh.

---

x   Phil. 2:7, according to the Latin Vulgate.

y   Luther here paraphrases the Latin Vulgate of Eph. 4:28. The Vulgate reads: "Let [the former thief] labor by working with his hands, which is a good thing, so that he may have a source from which he might contribute to the one who suffers need."

z   Luther was combining images from Rom. 14 and 1 Cor. 8–9, 12.

one another's burdens and so fulfilling the law of Christ."[a] Look here! This is truly the Christian life; here truly "faith is effective through love."[108] That is, with joy and love [faith] reveals itself in work of freest servitude, as one person, abundantly filled with the completeness and richness of his or her own faith, serves another freely and willingly.

### The Christian Life

Thus, after Paul had taught the Philippians how they were made rich through faith in Christ (in which faith they had obtained all things), he then teaches them by saying, "If then there is any encouragement in Christ, any consolation from love, any sharing in the Spirit, any compassion and sympathy, make my joy complete: be of the same mind, having the same love, being in full accord and of one mind. Do nothing from selfish ambition or conceit but in humility regard others as better than yourselves. Let each of you look not to your own interests but to the interests of others."[b] Here we see clearly that the Apostle places the life of Christians into this framework,[c] so that all of our works may be ordered toward the advantage of others. Since each and every person thus thrives through their own faith—so that all other works and the sum total of life flows out from that very faith—by these works each may serve and benefit the neighbor with willing benevolence. To this end, Paul introduces Christ as an example, stating: "Let the same mind be in you that was also in Christ Jesus, who, though he was in the form of God, did not regard himself to be equal to God, but emptied himself, taking the form of a servant, made in human likeness, and being found in human vesture . . . became obedient to the point of death."[d]

108. Luther's own rendering of Gal. 5:6. The Vulgate's "faith which works through love" (*fides per charitatem operatur*) led to the medieval insistence that love (*caritas*) provided the (Aristotelian) "form" for the material of faith. Luther not only uses the word *efficax* ("efficacious") but also, following Erasmus, *dilectio* ("ardent love") for *caritas*. See his discussion of this verse in the commentary on Galatians (1519) in LW 27:335–36.

---

a  Gal. 6:2.
b  Phil. 2:1-4. This precedes the biblical text on which the original sermon may have been based. See p. 489, n. 58.
c  Latin: *regula* (rule).
d  Phil. 2:5-8, according to the Vulgate.

**109.** The christological interpretation of Phil. 2 was standard from the time of the ancient church. Luther here is complaining that applying this verse only to the doctrine of Christ's two natures loses sight of its relation to the life of faith.

*Perverters of Apostolic Teaching*

To be sure, those who have completely misunderstood the apostolic vocabulary ("form of God," "form of a servant," "vesture," "human likeness") and have transferred it to the divine and human natures [of Christ] have obscured for us this most salutary word of the Apostle—even though Paul wanted to say the following.[109] Although Christ was filled with "the form of God" and abounded in all good things—so that he required no work or suffering in order to be righteous and saved (for he possessed all these things right from the very beginning)—nevertheless he was not puffed up by these things nor did he raise himself above us and arrogate to himself some kind of power over us, even though he could by rights have done so. But he acted contrary to this: living, working, suffering, and dying just like other humans, and in "vesture" and action he was nothing other than a human being, as if he lacked all of these things and possessed nothing of God's "forms." Yet he did all of this for our sake, in order to serve us and in order that all things that he had accomplished in the "form of a servant" might become ours.

*Let the Christian Be Conformed to Christ*

As Christ, their head, was rich and full through his faith, so each and every Christian ought to be content with this "form of God" obtained through faith, except that (as I have said) this very faith ought to increase until it is made perfect. For this faith is one's life, righteousness, and salvation: preserving and making each person acceptable and giving the Christian all things that Christ possesses, as stated above.[e] Paul also confirms this in Gal. 2[:20] when he says, "And the life I now live in the flesh I live by faith in the Son of God." Although individual Christians[f] are thereby free from all works, they should nevertheless once again "humble themselves" in this freedom, take on "the form of a servant," "be made in human form and found in human vesture," and serve, help, and do everything for their neighbor, just as they

e    See p. 499.

f    Singular in the original throughout this paragraph.

**Paſſional Chriſti vnd**

**Antichriſti.**

*Chriſtus.*

Szo ich ewre fueſze habe gewaſchen ð ich ewir her vñ meyſter bin/ vill mehr ſolt yr einander vnter euch die fuſze waſchen. Hie mit habe ich euch ein antzeygung vñ beyſpiel geben/ wie ich ym than habe/ alſzo ſolt yr hinfur auch thuen. Warlich warlich ſage ich euch/ ð knecht iſt nicht mehr dan ſeyn herre/ ſzo iſt auch nicht ð geſchickte botte mehr bñ ð yn geſandt hat/ Wiſt yr das! Selig ſeyt yr ſzo yr das thuen werdent. Johan. 13.

*Antichriſtus.*

Der Babſt maſt ſich an itzlichen Tyrannien vnd heydniſchen fürſten/ ſzo yre fueſz den leuten zu kuſzen dar gereiche/ nach zu volgen/ damit es waer werde das geſchrieben iſt. Wilcher dieſer beſtien bilde nicht anbettet/ſall getöd werden. Apocalip. 13. Diß kuſſens darff ſich der Babſt yn ſeynē decretalen vnnot ſchembt rümen. c. cū oli de pñ. cle. Si ſummus pon. de ſen. eᵗcō.

Jesus washing his disciples' feet contrasted with the pope's feet being kissed from the Passion of Christ and Antichrist (1521). See also pp. 417–18.

see God has done and does with them through Christ. And they should do this freely, having regard for nothing except divine approval.

### Christian Trust

Moreover, a Christian should think as follows: "Although I am unworthy and condemned, in Christ my God devotes to my insignificant person, without any merit and by sheer gracious mercy, all the riches of righteousness and salvation, so that I need absolutely nothing else further except faith, which believes that it is so. Thus, to such a Father as this, who overwhelms me with these his inestimable riches, why should I not freely, joyfully, with a whole heart and willing eagerness do everything that I know is pleasing and acceptable to him? Therefore, I will give myself as a kind of Christ to my neighbor, just as Christ offered himself to me. I will do nothing in this life except what I see will be necessary, advantageous, and salutary for my neighbor, because through faith I am overflowing with all good things in Christ."

### The Fruits of Faith (See, My Reader, How Worthily Luther Is Condemned!)[110]

Look at what love and joy in the Lord[g] flow from faith! Moreover, from love proceeds a joyful, gladsome, and free soul,[111] prepared for willing service to the neighbor, which takes no account of gratitude or ingratitude, praise or blame, profit or loss. For such a soul does not do this so that people may be obligated to it, nor does it distinguish between friends and enemies, nor does it anticipate thankfulness or ingratitude. Instead, it expends itself and what it has in a completely free and happy manner, whether squandering these things on the ungrateful or on the deserving. For as its Father also does—distributing everything to all people abundantly and freely and making "his sun to rise on the evil and on the good,"[h] so the son [or daughter] only does or suffers everything with spontaneous joy, as each person has through Christ been filled with delight in God, the lavish dispenser of all things.

*Recognizing How Great the Things Given to Us Are*
Therefore, you see that if we recognize those great and precious things that have been given to us, then, as Paul says, "love . . . is poured out in our hearts through the . . . Spirit."[i] By this love we are free, joyful, all-powerful workers and victors over all tribulations, servants of our neighbors and, nev-

**110.** The papal bull threatening excommunication, *Exsurge Domine*, condemned Luther for saying that the righteous sin in all their good works. See *Defense and Explanation of All the Articles* (1521) in LW 32:83–87.

**111.** Luther does not usually use this word to designate some more spiritual, less material part of the human being, but as a way of talking about the entire human creature standing before God. See p. 489, n. 59 above.

g   See Phil. 4:4.
h   Matt. 5:45.
i   Rom. 5:5.

ertheless, still lords of all.[j] But for all who do not recognize what has been given to them through Christ, Christ was born in vain, and such people carry on using works, never attaining a taste or sense of the things just described. Therefore, just as our neighbor has need and lacks what we have in abundance, so also we had need before God and lacked God's mercy. For this reason, as our heavenly Father supported us freely in Christ, so also we ought freely to support our neighbor with our body and its actions, and each person ought to become to the other a kind of Christ, so that we may be Christs to one another and be the same Christ in all, that is, truly Christians!

### The Glory of the Christian Life

Therefore, who can comprehend the riches and glory of the Christian life? It can do all things and has all things and lacks nothing. It is lord of sin, death, and hell but, at the same time, is servant and obedient and beneficial to all.[112] And yet how terrible it is that in our day this life is unknown! It is neither preached about nor sought after.

### Why We Are Called Christians

What is more, we are also completely ignorant of our very name, why we are Christians and bear that name. Without a doubt we are named after Christ—not absent from us but dwelling in us; in other words: provided that we believe in him and that, in turn and mutually, we are a second Christ to one another, doing for our neighbors as Christ does for us.[k] But nowadays, using human doctrines,[l] we are taught to seek nothing but merits, rewards, and the things that are ours, and we have made out of Christ nothing but a slave driver far harsher than Moses.[113, m]

**112.** For this contrast, see p. 488f.

**113.** Luther, following John 1:17, often contrasted "Moses" to Christ as harsh lawgiver to gracious savior. He did not, however, think that there was no grace in the "books of Moses" (Genesis through Deuteronomy). See, e.g., *How Christians Should Regard Moses* (1525) in LW 35:161–74.

j   See above, p. 488.
k   See Matt. 7:12 and John 13:34.
l   See Mark 7:7.
m   Latin: *exactor*.

**114.** Although rejecting the notion that Mary should be worshiped, Luther often pointed to Mary as an example of faith. See his *Commentary on the Magnificat* (written at Wartburg and published in 1522) in LW 21:297–358 and his exposition of the Ave Maria (Hail, Mary) in the *Personal Prayer Book* (1522) in LW 43:39–41. The marginal gloss uses the equivalent of *theotokos*, "Divine God-bearer" (*diva Dei genitrix*).

**115.** In this section of his argument, Luther provides a series of biblical examples to prove his point.

**116.** Luther held that Mary had herself conceived Jesus of the Holy Spirit without sin. Thus, she had no need of any purifying sacrifice.

**117.** Luther uses here a medieval term for court judges, *iustitiarii*, which contains within it the Latin word for righteousness (*iustitia*).

**118.** Luther uses the term *Magister*, which means teachers in general but in medieval Latin more specifically designated those Scholastic "masters" of theology. Luther takes up Romans 14 on p. 534.

### *The Holy Mother of God as an Example of Faith*[114]

The blessed Virgin provides a preeminent example[115] of this very faith, when (as is written in Luke 2[:22]) she was purified "according to the Law of Moses," as was the custom of all women. Although she was not bound by such a law and had no need of purification,[116] nevertheless, she subjected herself to the law out of free and voluntary love, doing just as other women did, so that she did not offend or disdain them. She was therefore not justified by this work, but as one already righteous, she did it freely and spontaneously. So also our works ought not be done for the purpose of being justified, since—already justified by faith—we ought to do all things freely and joyfully for the sake of others.

### *Paul Teaches Works*

St. Paul also circumcised his disciple Timothy,[n] not because circumcision was necessary for righteousness but rather so that he would not offend or disdain the Jews who were weak in faith and who could not yet grasp faith's freedom. However, on the contrary, when in contempt of this freedom of faith they insisted upon circumcision as necessary for righteousness, he resisted and did not permit Titus to be circumcised (Gal. 2[:3]). For just as he did not want to offend or disdain any person's weakness in faith, yielding to their wishes as appropriate, so also he did not want the freedom of faith to be offended against or disdained by hardened "justices."[117] He took a middle course, sparing the weak as appropriate and always resisting the hardened, so that he might convert everyone to the freedom of faith. Our actions also ought to be done with the same devotion, so that we support the weak in faith (as Rom. 14[:1] teaches) but resist boldly the hardened "masters" of works, about which we will say more below.[118]

*n*   Acts 16:3.

### The Example of Christ the Lord

Moreover, in Matt. 17[:24-27], when a tax payment was demanded from the disciples, Christ discussed with Peter whether or not a king's sons were exempt from paying taxes. But when Peter affirmed that they were exempt, Jesus nevertheless commanded him to go to the sea, saying [v. 27]: "However, so that we do not give offense to them, go to the sea and cast a hook; take the first fish that comes up; and when you open its mouth you will find a coin; take that and give it to them for you and me." This example beautifully supports our argument,[119] in that Christ refers to himself and his own as free sons of the king, who need nothing, and yet he willingly submits and pays the tax. As little as this deed was necessary or useful for righteousness or salvation, so all of his other works and those of his followers contribute nothing to righteousness, since all of these things are a result of righteousness and free, done only as an example and a service to others.

### Let All the Religious Understand and Let Luther Be Your Teacher[o]

The same thing goes for what Paul commands in Rom. 13[:1] and Titus 3[:1], saying, "Let" them "be subject to the governing authorities" and "be ready for every good work"—not that they may be justified through this (since they are already justified by faith) but so that through these things and in the freedom of the Spirit they may serve the authorities, among others, and may obey them out of willing, spontaneous love. The works of all clerical institutions,[120] monasteries, and priests should be of this kind, too. Thus, each would only do works of his own profession and walk of life,[121] in order to work not toward righteousness but, in the first place, toward the subjection of his own body as an example for the sake of others, who have need to discipline their own bodies, too. In the second place, they would

119. A *propositio* meant either the theme of a speech or the major premise of a logic syllogism.

120. Literally, "colleges," a designation for legally constituted groups of clergy supported by a foundation or cathedral for the purpose of performing certain religious observances.

121. Luther uses the Latin *status* here as a synonym for the German *stand*, "station in life" or "walk of life."

o   Latin: *religiosi*, a technical term encompassing the ordained (priests and bishops) and those under a vow (monks, nuns, and friars).

also obey others and do their bidding out of spontaneous love. Nevertheless, here the utmost care must be taken, so that a false trust does not presume that such works justify, earn reward, or save—which is all from faith alone, as I have repeatedly said.

## A True Christian's Knowledge

Therefore, whoever has this knowledge can easily and without danger manage those countless rules and commands of the pope, bishops, monasteries, churches, princes, and magistrates. Some foolish shepherds[p] insist that these things are all necessary for righteousness and salvation, calling them "commands of the church,"[122] although they are nothing of the kind. For a free Christian will say instead, "I will fast, pray, and do this or that because it is commanded by human beings—not because this is necessary for righteousness or salvation but because in this behavior I may conduct myself toward the pope, bishop, community, this or that magistrate, or my neighbor as an example. I will do or suffer all things, as Christ often did and suffered many things for me—none of which he needed for himself at all, having been "placed under the law" on my account, although he was not under the law.[q] And although tyrants may harm or use force [to effect compliance], it will still not do harm, as long as [what they commanded] was not against God."[123]

### Distinguishing Good Shepherds from Evil Ones

From all these examples,[124, r] any person can derive firm judgment and reliable distinction among all works and laws and can recognize who are the blind, foolish shepherds and who are the true and good ones. For any work not directed toward the purpose of either disciplining the body

122. For example, this phrase occurs in Thomas Aquinas, *Summa Theologica* II/II q. 39 a. 1, ad 2 (a discussion of schism in the church), but it was more commonly used in moral theology, which listed five or six precepts of the church that must be followed. Lists might include receiving the Lord's Supper during the Easter season, following appointed fasts, supporting the church monetarily, obeying the church's marriage laws, hearing the Mass on Sundays and holy days, and going to private confession yearly.

123. This double attitude toward authority is reflected in Luther's letter to Pope Leo X, toward whom he tries to demonstrate both obedience and freedom (see above, p. 468). Later he applies this respect toward and limits of authority to secular authority as well. See *On Secular Authority* (1523) in LW 45:81–129.

124. There are four examples beginning with Mary.

p  Latin: *pastores*.

q  Some modern versions end the quotation here. Quotation marks were not employed in sixteenth-century printings. The reference is to Gal. 4:4-5.

r  Literally, "things."

or serving the neighbor (as long as the neighbor demands nothing against God) is neither good nor Christian. As a result, I greatly fear that nowadays few if any clerical institutions, monasteries, high altars,[125] or ecclesiastical offices are Christian, along with special fasts and prayers for certain saints. To repeat, I fear that in all of these things nothing is sought after except what has to do with us, because we think that through them our sins are cleansed and salvation is attained. In this way, Christian freedom is completely obliterated, because [this attitude] arises from ignorance of Christian faith and freedom.

Many completely blind shepherds zealously support such ignorance and suppression of freedom, while at the same time inciting and encouraging the people in their devotion by praising these things and inflating them with indulgences,[126] and yet never teaching faith at all.

### Advice

Instead, I desire each of you to consider that if you really want to pray, fast, or establish a foundation in churches (as they say),[127] pay attention to whether you are doing it for the purpose of obtaining some temporal or eternal reward!

### Be Concerned for Faith Alone

You may harm your faith, which alone offers you all things. For this reason, let faith be your sole concern, so that faith may be increased by exercising it either through works or suffering. Meanwhile, whatever you give, give freely and without reward, so that others may experience increase and reap benefits from you and what is yours. For in this way, you will be truly good and Christian. For what are your good works (which function most fully for bodily discipline) to you, when for yourself you are filled through your faith, in which God gives you all things?[s]

125. Latin: *altaria*. Luther is probably referring to altars reserved for saying Masses for the dead.

126. In late medieval piety and connected with the sacrament of penance, many works, such as special fasts, prayers, or pilgrimages, were made even more meritorious with the addition of specially crafted indulgences. These limited indulgences, designed to encourage a variety of works, differed in scope from the plenary "Peter's Indulgence," which Luther attacks in the *95 Theses*. See above, p. 15f.

127. Luther is referring to the practice of establishing monetary foundations so priests could recite perpetual Masses for one's deceased family members.

---

s  Luther uses the word *you* (singular: *tu*) five times in this sentence, including *pro te* ("for you").

**128.** Luther is alluding to the baptismal language of "taking off" and "putting on" found in Col. 3:1-17.

**129.** Luther reworks the "joyous exchange" (see above, p. 499f.) to describe relations between the believer and the neighbor.

**130.** This verb begins the concluding section of Luther's tract, similar to the peroration in good Latin rhetoric of the time. It summarizes the chief argument, introduced on p. 488.

**131.** The *Postilla moralis* of Nicholas of Lyra (1270-1349), provides a similar allegory, in that preachers ascend to the deity of Christ and descend "when they seek the need of the neighbor raised up for their love." For a different interpretation of this text by Luther, in sermons from 1538, see LW 22:200-211.

### The Rule for "Brotherly Love"

Look here! This should be the rule: that the good things we have from God may flow from one person to the other and become common property. In this way each person may "put on" his [or her] neighbor[128] and conduct oneself toward him [or her] as if in the neighbor's place. These good things flowed and flow into us from Christ, who put us on and acted for us, as if he himself were what we are. They now flow from us into those who have need of them. Just as my faith and righteousness ought to be placed before God to cover and intercede for the neighbor's sins, which I take upon myself, so also I labor under and am subject to them as if they were my very own.[129] For this is what Christ did for us. For this is true love and the genuine rule of the Christian life. Now where there is true and genuine faith, there is true and genuine love. Hence, the Apostle in 1 Cor. 13[:5] attributes to love that "it does not seek its own." [t]

### The Christian Lives in Christ and the Neighbor

Therefore, we conclude[130] that Christian individuals[u] do not live in themselves but in Christ and their neighbor, or else they are not Christian. They live in Christ through faith and in the neighbor through love. Through faith they are caught up beyond themselves into God; likewise through love they fall down beneath themselves into the neighbor—remaining nevertheless always in God and God's love, as Christ says in John 1[:51]: "Very truly I say to you, you will see the heavens opened and the angels of God ascending and descending upon the Son of Man."[131]

Let this suffice concerning that freedom, which, as you see, is spiritual and true, making our hearts free from all sin, laws, and commands, as Paul says in 1 Tim. 1[:9], "The law is not laid down for the righteous person." [v] This freedom is

---

*t*     Following here the more literal Latin Vulgate.

*u*     This is singular in the original throughout this paragraph.

*v*     A literal rendering of the Latin Vulgate and the Greek text.

far above all other external freedoms, as high as heaven is above the earth. May Christ cause us to know and preserve this freedom! Amen.

### [Appendix][132]Against the Freedom of the Flesh[w]

Finally, this must be added because of those for whom nothing can be stated well enough that they cannot distort it by warped understanding—if they could even understand what is said here at all. There are so many people who, when they hear about this freedom of faith, immediately turn it into "an occasion for the flesh."[x] They imagine that straightaway all things are permitted for them, and they want to be free and seem Christian in no other way than by showing contempt and disdain for ceremonies,[y] traditions, and human laws. As if they were Christians precisely because they do not fast on the stated days or because they themselves eat meat while others fast[133] or they refrain from saying the customary prayers! They stick up their noses, make fun of human commands, and hold the other things that in fact pertain to the Christian religion in low esteem.

### Against Trust in Works

These people are stubbornly resisted by those who strive for salvation solely by reverent observance of ceremonies—as if they might be saved because they fast on the appointed days or abstain from meat or pray certain prayers. They boast about the precepts of the church and the Fathers while not caring one wit about those things that concern our genuine faith. Both sides are plainly in error, because they are so confused and troubled about unnecessary and silly things while neglecting the more serious things that are necessary for salvation.

**132.** This marginal word is not in sixteenth-century editions, which simply put a larger space between the preceding and what follows. This appendix, found only in the Latin edition, deals with a persistent charge against Luther and his followers: that their understanding of Christian freedom resulted only in license to sin and, hence, fostered civil disobedience. Dealing with this issue also gives Luther opportunity to attack what he views as his opponents' legalism. Thus, each section, as the marginal notations from the second edition help make clear, deals with both sides of the problem. The Latin here is somewhat more complicated than the preceding, perhaps because of the absence of a German text.

**133.** In late medieval practice, people were to abstain from meat on certain days (especially Fridays) and seasons (especially Lent)—religious regulations enforced by local authorities. In 1523 in Zurich, eating of meat during Lent by a prominent printer led to the wholesale rejection of episcopal authority and the establishment of an important center for what became Reformed Christianity.

---

w   "Against the Freedom of the Flesh" is from the 2nd ed.

x   Gal. 5:13 according to the Vulgate and Greek text. NRSV: "an opportunity for self-indulgence."

y   For Luther's use of this word throughout this section, see above, p. 494, n. 68.

How much more correct is the Apostle Paul, who teaches taking the middle way and condemns both sides completely when he says, "Those who eat must not despise those who abstain, and those who abstain must not pass judgment on those who eat."[z] You see here that those who neglect or despise ceremonies—not out of a sense of piety but rather out of sheer contempt—are upbraided, since Paul teaches not to condemn, for "knowledge puffs them up."[a] On the other hand, he teaches those other, obstinate people not to judge the former group. For neither side cares about the "love that builds up" the neighbor.[b] Therefore, Scripture must be listened to, which teaches that we "will turn aside neither to the right nor to the left"[c] but will follow "the acceptable righteousness of the Lord that gladdens the heart."[d] For just as no one is righteous by preserving or being a slave to the works and rites of ceremonies, so also no one is deemed righteous by simply omitting and condemning them.

For we are not free from works through faith in Christ but from conjectures about works, that is, from the foolish presumption of justification acquired through works. For faith redeems, makes right, and guards our consciences, so that we realize that righteousness is not in works—although works can and should not be lacking. For example, we cannot exist without food and drink and all the other works of this mortal body, and yet our righteousness is not built upon them but upon faith. Still these things must not be condemned or omitted. Thus, in this world we are bound by the necessities of this bodily life, but we are not righteous because of them. Christ said, "My kingdom is not from this world . . . not from here," but he did not say, "My kingdom is not here in this world."[e] Paul also says, "For though we walk

z    Rom. 14:3.
a    Paraphrasing 1 Cor. 8:1.
b    Paraphrasing 1 Cor. 8:1.
c    Paraphrasing Deut. 2:27 and 28:14.
d    Paraphrasing Ps. 19:8.
e    John 18:36.

in the flesh, we do not war according to the flesh."*f* And in Gal. 2[:20] he says, "The life I now live in the flesh I live by faith in the Son of God." Thus, the necessities of life and the need to control the body cause us to act and live and exist with works and ceremonies. Nevertheless, we are righteous not through these things but through faith in the Son of God. For this reason, the same middle way is set out for each Christian, who must also keep in mind these two types of people.

### How to Deal with the Stubborn

On the one hand, the Christian encounters the stubborn and obstinate ceremonialists. Like deaf adders,*g* they do not want to hear freedom's truth, but instead they boast about their ceremonies as the means of justification, imperiously commanding and insisting on them quite apart from faith. The Jews of old, who did not want to understand anything about how to behave properly, were like this.[134] Against these people one ought to resist, do the opposite, and boldly offend them, so that they do not mislead many others as well by this ungodly opinion. In their presence it is appropriate to eat meat, to break fasts, and for the freedom of faith to do other things that they take for the greatest of sins. It must be said of them, "Let them alone; they are blind guides of the blind."*h* In line with this, Paul did not want Titus to be circumcised when some demanded it,*i* and Christ defended the apostles because they wanted [to pluck] grain on the Sabbath and in many other instances.*j*

134. As what follows makes clear, Luther had in mind conflicts between Jesus and the Pharisees over keeping the law. See, e.g., Mark 2:1—3:6.

---

*f*   2 Cor. 10:3, using the more literal rendering of the Greek, which matches the Latin Vulgate.

*g*   Ps. 58:4 (see also Mic. 7:16-17).

*h*   Matt. 15:14.

*i*   Gal. 2:3.

*j*   Matt. 12:1-8.

135. A reference to Luther's Roman opponents, especially the priests and bishops.

### Regarding the Common Folk

On the other hand, the Christian encounters the simple, uneducated, ignorant, and (as Paul calls them) weak in faith, who cannot yet understand this freedom of faith, even if they want to. Care must be taken not to offend these people but to defer to their weakness until they are more fully instructed. For fasts and other things that they think are necessary must be kept to avoid causing them to fall—not because their actions or thoughts are motivated by deep-seated wickedness but only because they are weak in faith. For love, which seeks to harm no one but only to serve all, demands it. After all, they are weak not by their own fault but by that of their shepherds,[135] who have taken them captive and wickedly beaten them using the snares and rods of their traditions, from which they should have been freed and healed with the teaching of faith and freedom! As the Apostle teaches in [1 Cor. 8:13],[k] "I will never eat meat, so that I may not cause one of them to fall." And he says elsewhere, "I know and am persuaded by the Lord Jesus that nothing is unclean . . . but to anyone who thinks it is unclean . . . [and] it is evil for that person who eats to give offense."[l]

### Concerning Laws and the Lawgivers

Therefore, although those master teachers of traditions must be boldly resisted and the papal laws, by which they plunder God's people, must be sharply criticized, nevertheless one must refrain from injuring the frightened masses—which those ungodly tyrants hold captive with these very laws—until they may be set free from them. Thus, fight vigorously against the wolves but *for* the sheep and not, in the same breath, against the sheep. Each of you may do this by inveighing against the laws and the lawgivers while at the same time guarding the weak from being offended, until

---

k   The original text refers to Romans 14, the passage Luther cites next.
l   Rom. 14:14, 20, where Luther cites the Vulgate, which provides a more literal rendering of the Greek.

they themselves recognize this tyranny and understand their own freedom. If you desire to exercise your freedom, do it in secret, as Paul says in Rom. 14[:22], "The faith that you have, have for yourself before God." *m* But be careful not to exercise [faith's freedom] before the weak. Contrariwise, before tyrants and stubborn people you may exercise that freedom with contempt and without ever letting up at all. Then they, too, will understand that they are ungodly, that their laws contribute nothing to righteousness, and that, frankly, they did not even have the right to enact them.

### For the Young and Untrained

Thus, it is clear that in this life one cannot live without ceremonies and works. Indeed, hotheaded and untrained adolescents need to be held back and guarded by such restraints. Moreover, individual Christians must discipline their bodies with such efforts. The servant of Christ *n* must be wise and faithful, so that he may so rule and teach Christ's people about all these things, so that their conscience and faith are not offended. Otherwise, an opinion or "root of bitterness" may arise in them "and through it many become defiled," as Paul warns in Heb. [12:15].[136] That is to say, "so that, in the absence of faith, they begin to be defiled by the opinion about works, as if they were justified through them." This happens quite easily and defiles many people. Unless faith is constantly inculcated at the same time, it is impossible to avoid the situation where (faith having been silenced) human regulations alone are taught. This has happened today through the pestilent, ungodly, soul-destroying, traditions of our popes and the opinions of our theologians.[137] With an infinite number of souls being dragged to hell by these snares, you can recognize Antichrist.[138]

**136.** In the sixteenth century, biblical interpreters debated whether Paul wrote Hebrews. Luther was of a divided mind on the subject but here supports the traditional viewpoint.

**137.** See above, *Address to the Christian Nobility*, p. 430.

**138.** Luther uses the widespread depiction of the devil, who at the end of time binds the souls of the damned around the neck and leads them into hell. By this stage of the Reformation, Luther was convinced that the Antichrist ruled in Rome and was associated with the institution of the Roman papacy. See, e.g., *On the Papacy in Rome against the Most Celebrated Romanist in Leipzig* (1520), in LW 39:49–104.

*m* Following Luther's citation of the Vulgate, which renders the Greek more literally.

*n* Latin: *minister Christi*, Luther's favorite designation for the public minister.

### Danger in Ceremonies

In conclusion, just as riches endanger poverty; business dealings, honesty; honors, humility; banquets, abstinence; or pleasures, chastity; so also ceremonies endanger the righteousness of faith. Solomon asks, "Can fire be carried in the bosom without burning one's clothes?"[o] And yet, as with riches, business dealings, honors, pleasures, and feasts, so also one must take part in ceremonies—that is, in dangers. To say this as strongly as possible:[p] Just as infant boys need to be attentively caressed at a young woman's bosom, in order that they may not perish (even though as adults it endangers salvation for them to be consorting with young women), so also hotheaded, untrained youth need to be restrained and disciplined by the iron bars of ceremonies, so that their unrestrained heart may not go blindly into corruption. And yet it would be the death of them if they insisted on imagining that justification came from them. Instead, they should be taught that they have been imprisoned in this way not to be righteous or to merit something but so that they would be kept from evil and might more easily be instructed in the righteousness of faith. For, unless their impulsiveness be put in check, they would not put up with such instruction.

### The Place for Ceremonies

Thus, ceremonies are to have the same place in the Christian life as a builder's construction plans or an artisan's instructions. They are not prepared to be the substance and lasting part of a building but because without them nothing can be built or made. For they are set aside once the structure is finished. Here you can see that they are not being despised but rather are especially required. What is being despised is a [false] opinion about them: because no one imagines that plans are the real and permanent structure. Who would be so silly that they would care for nothing in life other than

---

o    Prov. 6:27.

p    Latin: *immo*, an adversative much beloved by Luther, who used it to introduce radical or even contrary ideas from what had just been stated. It is similar to the archaic "forsooth" or "nay, verily."

plans that they had most lavishly, carefully, and stubbornly[q] prepared while never thinking about the structure itself and only being pleased with and boasting about their work in making plans and such vain first steps? Would not everybody have pity on such insanity and judge that something great could have been built by this wasted expense? In the same way, we do not despise ceremonies or works but rather especially require them. However, we despise the [false] opinion about works, so that a person may not imagine that they are true righteousness, as hypocrites do. They waste their whole life by tying their life to works, and yet they never arrive at the goal for which works are done. As the Apostle says, they "are always being instructed and can never arrive at knowledge of the truth."[r] For it seems that they want to build and to prepare themselves and yet never actually build anything. So they remain with "the outward form of godliness and do not" attain "its power."[s]

### On Hyper-Religious[t] People

All the while these people are pleased with their efforts and dare to judge everyone else whom they do not see glowing with a similar display of works. Instead, had they been filled with faith, by properly using God's gifts (rather than vainly wasting and abusing them) they could have brought about great things for their salvation and the salvation of others. But human nature and natural reason (as they call it)[139] are naturally hyper-religious and, whenever some laws and works are proposed, promptly jump to the conclusion that justification may be attained through them. Added to this, reason is trained and strengthened in this very point of view by the practice of all earthly lawgivers. Therefore, it

139. This term went back to Cicero and was a central concept in Roman law.

q Latin: *pertinacissime*. In this context, Luther means "meticulously," but he is using the same word that he had already used to describe "*stubborn*" ceremonialists."

r 2 Tim. 3:7.

s 2 Tim. 3:5.

t Here and below *superstitiosus* (here translated "hyper-religious") means fixed on one's own unreasonable ideas about religion.

is impossible that by its own powers [reason] may free itself from servitude to this view of works and come into the necessary knowledge of faith's freedom. For this reason, prayer is needed, so that the Lord may "draw us" and make us "*theo-didaktos*," that is, "taught by God."*ᵘ* Moreover, as he promised, he will "write the law in our hearts."*ᵛ* Otherwise, it is all over for us. For unless God teaches this wisdom hidden in mystery*ʷ* inwardly, [human] nature, because it is offended and regards it as foolish, can only condemn it and judge it to be heretical.*ˣ* What we observe happened to the prophets and Apostles, those godless and blind pontiffs and their flatterers are now doing to me and people like me. In the end, "may God be merciful to us . . . and cause his face to shine upon us, so that we may know his way on earth, among all nations the saving power of the one"*ʸ* who is blessed forever. Amen.

*u*    Luther is quoting John 6:44-45, mixing the Latin and Greek text.
*v*    Jer. 31:33.
*w*    See Col. 1:26.
*x*    See 1 Cor. 1:23.
*y*    A close paraphrase of Ps. 67:1-2.

# Image Credits

466, 479, 483, 509, 513, 517: Courtesy of the Digital Image Archive,
Pitts Theology Library, Candler School of Theology, Emory University.